Own Your Goals:
The Ultimate Guide to Setting, Sticking to and Achieving Your Biggest Life Goals

KASSANDRA VAUGHN

DISCLAIMER

Own Your Goals: The Ultimate Guide to Setting, Sticking to and Achieving Your Biggest Life Goals

Copyright © 2023 by **SK Media LLC**

CONTENTS

YOUR THREE FREE GIFTS

I so appreciate that you invested in the purchase of this book and that you're taking the time to read it. In the spirit of gratitude, I'd like to offer you three free gifts that are exclusive to my book and blog readers (you won't find this offer anywhere else).

The first free gift is **The Top 10 Life Goals Workbook**, a powerful resource guide that will help you get clear on your top ten life goals. If you're looking for a step-by-step guide for deciding and committing to your biggest life goals, this is it!

To grab your copy of **The Top 10 Life Goals Workbook**, go https://kassandravaughn.lpages.co/top10lifegoals/.

Your next gift is **Bet on You: A Guide to Building Goal Self-Belief**, a mindset guide designed to help you grow your level of self-belief so you can go after AND achieve your goals. If you're ready to have access to a variety of self-belief development strategies that will help you with goal decision, strategy and follow-through, this is the guide for you!

To grab your copy of **Bet on You: A Guide to Building Goal Self-Belief**, go to: https://kassandravaughn.lpages.co/growyourgoalselfbelief/.

Your third gift is a powerful tip sheet called **7 Simple Ways to Be More Consistent**. If you're looking for a quick, effective guide to developing your focus and consistency muscles, this is it!

To grab your copy of **7 Simple Ways to Be More Consistent**, go to https://kassandravaughn.lpages.co/consistency7ways/.

INTRODUCTION

Sometimes, we need to be brave enough to outgrow the life we've built.
- Unknown

I remember one of the first times I failed to hit a major goal. I was a sophomore in college, pre-med, and was taking an EMT certification course. As a pre-med student, I knew that becoming a certified EMT, while in college, would look really good on a medical school application… only… deep down, I didn't really want to be a doctor, hated the sight of blood, and struggled immensely with organic chemistry and anything related to math. But, I was doing what I thought was the right next step… and passing my EMT certification was a key part of that.

So the day came when it was time to pass both the physical and written EMT exams. It's been so many years, I can't recall which test I failed but I failed one of them… and it was the first time I'd really failed anything in my life. Having started college at 16, I was used to being an overachiever… and here I was… having failed a piece of the EMT certification path and realizing that I only had one more chance to get it right or I wouldn't become an EMT.

I went back to my dorm room, closed the shades, and cried. I spent a number of days in bed, lying in a fetal position, the covers over my head, not wanting to see or hear from anyone. I fell into a deep depression and didn't respond to phone calls or messages, not even from my EMT instructor who encouraged me to try again. He didn't want to fail me in the class or see me not finish the certification. He left message after message and I didn't respond to any of them.

At the end of the day, I failed the EMT certification and I failed the EMT class… all because I was afraid to try again. I didn't want my inability to succeed the first time confirmed to me. I didn't want to have to work so hard to achieve something that, deep down, I knew wasn't for me. I didn't want to have to figure out how to get around the obstacles I was facing... and that was my first lesson in what it means to NOT own my goals.

I was pursuing a goal that wasn't really mine and that I actually did not want. I, for the first time, could not summon enough resolve to make myself do the thing I didn't want to do. In high school, it was easy to jump through the hoops I had to jump through: A- I wanted to go to college and B- The effort to make it through was minimal.

Failing this EMT class was the first time I had to face myself and acknowledge that I could no longer make myself do what, deep down, I knew wasn't for me. I was offended by my inability to force my way to achievement. I hated the fact that my authentic desire came through in my lack of investment. I was pursuing a goal that wasn't actually for me... which brings me to the focus of this book.

There have been hundreds, if not thousands, of books written on the topic of achieving goals. Throughout this book, I'll weave in various aspects from some of the goal-centered books that I love. But, what I still don't see, even in the goal achievement books I adore, is a book that goes into detail on not simply goal setting or goal achievement but on what it takes to OWN your goals. In other words, what it takes to successfully (and efficiently) manage your way to your goals, not because the goals you set are easy and not because the goals you set are hard but because the goals you set are FOR YOU.

It took me a VERY long time to understand the difference between a goal I COULD achieve and a goal I was meant to go after... and, once I figured that out, I found that owning my goals, being vigilantly committed to them, and staying the course UNTIL I achieved them became relatively easy... and that's what I'm going to teach in this book- how to determine the goals that are MEANT for you in this season of your life, how to set up your current life so it's easy to go after those goals, how to set boundaries that protect your goal focus time, and how to successfully take yourself from goal setting to goal achievement through focus and attention on **goal management.**

If you're ready to take a new approach to an ancient process, you're reading the right book. Let's get to it…

Thank you for purchasing **Own Your Goals: The Ultimate Guide to Setting, Sticking to and Achieving Your Biggest Goals.**

Kassandra

CHAPTER 1: THE FIRST AND MOST IMPORTANT STEP TO GOAL ACHIEVEMENT

The STRONGEST factor for success is self-belief: Believing you can do it, believing you deserve it, and believing you will get it.
- Unknown

Have you ever pursued a goal that felt impossible to achieve? You want it more than any other goal. You dream of achieving it and, yet, of all your goals, it is the ONE goal for which you have the smallest level of faith that you can actually make it happen. I'm in that place right now.

For more than a decade, I've longed to have more children. I've spent my entire adult life battling secondary infertility and, when I divorced at 29, I KNEW in my heart of hearts that I was not done having children. Fast forward fifteen years and I find myself, a few weeks away from my 45th birthday, still feeling the yearning of what I consider my biggest life goal and, yet, I find myself, after years of wishing, hoping, and trying, without the level of self-belief to take my efforts to the next level.

When I say I've tried to have more children, I can look back at my 30s and early 40s and see that I did a number of things to 'try': I read all the books on infertility. I consulted with different fertility coaches and doctors. I took three or four attempts at minimally invasive fertility treatments. But, did I go ALL IN on having more children? Did I, from my vantage point today, do everything in my power to make that happen? I can look back and say that I didn't… which leads me to the topic of this first chapter and a reckoning that, as I approach Year 45, I'm currently having with myself.

For every major life goal I've ever achieved, including having my 2nd child after four years of secondary infertility, the ONE thing that I did have, at some point along the goal journey, was BELIEF in my ability to transform the situation. Notice I didn't say "believe in my ability to achieve the goal."

When the goal was finishing my MBA as I was flunking Managerial Economics, yes, I had to shift my belief that I could finish that class and graduate with my MBA in order to do that. But, when it came to having my second baby after four years of nothing, it wasn't that I shifted my belief that I would get pregnant. It was that I stopped drowning myself in the hope and dashed dreams of not being pregnant with every passing month and pivoted my FULL belief and attention to a goal I could attain- losing 60 pounds and getting into the best shape of my life… which I did and then, just like that, I got pregnant and had my second baby.

I'm writing all of this because I, perhaps like you, am having a goal journey struggle. I'm sitting in a place where I feel like this goal of having more babies is going to come to an end in the next two or three years and I've been beating myself up about WHY I haven't done everything in my power to achieve that goal… and it comes back to the thing that I want to talk about in this chapter, the thing that, above and beyond everything else I'm going to teach you in this book, if you don't do this thing, none of the other strategies and techniques will work.

I haven't gone ALL IN on having more babies because, in my heart of hearts, **I don't believe in my body's ability to do so…** and it grieves me to write that and it pains me for that to be true… Only it is… and every fiber of my being wishes I could just flip a switch and make myself believe in my body's ability to conceive… except I don't AND I know that self-belief is, by far, the most important decider of whether I achieve the goal or not.

Can you relate?

It's brutal how little I believe in my body. It's brutal how little faith I have in my ability to turn this around. And it's really brutal that I've had this limiting belief for as long as I've been an adult. I can't blame it on being in my 40s or on the odds of conceiving at this point. I've always felt this way… until there were moments when I didn't. It was in those moments that I was able to conceive, carry and give birth to my children.

So I'm telling you all of this because there's something we need to get VERY clear on before doing any of the work contained in this book: **the cultivation of self-belief MUST come first…** and I'm going to lay out the approach that I'm taking to build my own level of self-belief in the area of having more children in my 40s so you can take this formula and apply it to the biggest goal or dream of your life.

Let's start with the WHY…

The first and most important step to goal achievement is your level of self-belief. Every thought you think, feeling you have, and action you take will be based on the extent to which you believe the outcome of those thoughts, feelings, and actions are leading to your goal being achieved. Why would you put in the necessary time, effort and energy into a goal you don't actually believe you'll ever attain? You wouldn't and you won't because, even if you can say all the right things and get yourself pumped up for the outcome, if, deep down, you don't really believe you can make it happen, you will subconsciously and unconsciously find ways to sabotage yourself.

And here's where people get the requirement of self-belief twisted. I'm not saying you have to have COMPLETE self-belief in your ability to achieve the goal. You simply have to have an anchor of self-belief that allows you to move forward in confidence that then gets built up as you go from one level of milestone achievement to the other.

Let's say your goal is to lose weight and you've never been able to lose and keep the weight off before. To expect you to jump from a history of yo-yo dieting to now feeling unstoppable when it comes to the goal of losing thirty pounds in six months is ludicrous. That won't work.

But… Can you start with stepping out on faith and saying to yourself "I BELIEVE that I'm the person who can put in the work of losing weight starting today. I BELIEVE that I can get at least 3,000 steps in each day and record everything I'm eating in MyFitnessPal for the next 30 days. I'm not going to ask myself to go on a diet right now. I'm not going to ask myself to work out 2 hours a day, six days a week right now. That's too far from where my self-belief is right now. But, I KNOW that if I say I'm going to do 3,000 steps a day and record everything I eat in MyFitnessPal for the next 30 days, I KNOW I can at least do that"? Could you start there?

It's not about leaping from a history of goal non-accomplishment or sustainment to a place of absolute faith that you can achieve the big goal. It's about finding a grain of self-belief contained within your biggest goal and holding on to that grain of faith UNTIL it becomes more...

In my fertility example, here's how I'm approaching shifting my level of self-belief:

> *Step #1: Radical acceptance of what is...*
> What is, right now, is that I don't believe in my body's ability to produce a baby with my own eggs. I don't and, rather than pretending that this isn't the case, I'm using radical acceptance to have compassion for where I am so I can say to myself "Okay, this is where I am. It's not going to be where I stay but I am acknowledging that, in this moment, this is where things are."

> *Step #2: Find your self-belief anchor...*
> I know I can't go from not believing in my ability to get pregnant to, all of a sudden, saying to myself "The statistics don't matter! I believe I can and will do this." No, I am not in a position to make that leap right now. What I can do, right now, is say to myself "Okay, so I don't have faith in my body, not only when it comes to getting pregnant but in general. How can I address that? I can lose this extra weight I'm carrying around and feel better about my body. In doing so, I'll feel more confident in its ability to work well... and then we'll get back to the fertility question." So, for me, what my intuition is deeply telling me is that I need to get my mind off of "How can I get pregnant?" and onto "How can I lose this weight so I improve my level of body confidence and, in doing so, put myself in a better position to improve and believe in my fertility?" Now the self-belief anchor shifts. It is no longer in achieving a goal I've struggled with all of my adult life. Now the self-belief anchor is in getting fit, a thing I've been able to accomplish numerous times across my adult lifespan. Do I still battle the "Once you're 40, your metabolism changes and it's harder to lose weight?" Yes, but that messaging is nowhere near as powerful in me as the limiting beliefs about my fertility. In my mind, I know that I've lost weight before and I can do it again-self-belief in place and ready to be accessed again.

➤ *Step #3: Releasing the desperation for the goal...*
This, too, is about self-belief. If my entire life rides on the goal of having more children and I never achieve that goal, then what is my entire life about? Nothing... While I don't want to release the goal and act as if it's okay that I never get there, I certainly want to practice surrendering the goal and saying to myself "What do I think having more children will give me in terms of quality of life, connection, and accomplishment that I can give to myself RIGHT NOW... well before those children show up?" I'm going to journal the answer to that question and then start LIVING the answers to those questions now. For example, I want more children because I want a different experience of motherhood. I want to raise this next batch of babies without the pain of divorce and custody battles and one parent brainwashing the children against the other. I want to focus my time and attention on my babies because I'm older, wiser, more present, and more able to help them live their purpose and do what they were put on this earth to do. But, you know what? I can be doing all of that right now without them even being here. I can mother through my coaching programs and working with clients. I can mother by mentoring and coaching my adult children who still need their mother to help them live their purpose and do what they were put on this earth to do. I can mother my second batch of babies by being consistent with my nightly Spirit Babies meditation and setting aside dedicated time to sit with my spirit babies and talk to them and tell them how much I love them, whether they choose to show up this lifetime or not. I could do all of those things and experience all of that connection right now. I don't have to wait for the goal to be achieved to do that. So, why wouldn't I? That's what it means to release the desperation for the goal. The releasing is actually an act of surrender.

➤ *Step #4: Staying in the step that I'm in...*
Staying in the step I'm in means doing the work of firmly establishing my self-belief anchor- no excuses, no delays and I put ALL of my focus on that. Again, could I focus on paying for more infertility treatments and going to see IVF doctors? Sure. But, the IVF doctor can't fix the fact that I currently don't believe in my

body; only I can do that. So I need to keep my focus on staying in the step that I'm in- which is losing the weight so I firm up my belief and confidence in my body's ability to work well.

Over the course of this book, I'm going to give practical, tactical strategies you can use to effectively set, manage and achieve your goals. Let me be VERY clear- none of those strategies will work if you don't have some level of self-belief that you CAN achieve the goals you set. If you're sitting in a place of recognition that you don't believe you can achieve the goals that you've set, it's time to do the four steps I've listed above... and let me go through them again...

Step #1: Radical Acceptance of What Is...

Call an ace an ace. If you don't believe, in this moment, that you can achieve the goal, tell yourself the truth about it. "I don't believe that I can achieve this goal... but I'm willing to figure out how to get to a place of self-belief." When you tell yourself the truth, you eliminate the heaviness of feeling like you're an imposter. Instead, you come to grips with the struggle that you have and you use the extra energy to explore possibilities for increasing your level of self-belief.

Step #2: Find Your Self-Belief Anchor

You don't believe in your ability to achieve the goal you set. What can you believe in that's somehow related to the achievement of that goal? What past successes or achievements can you pull from to increase your level of self-confidence and self-belief? How can you begin working towards the goal in a small way but in a way that builds your level of self-belief that you can make your way to the big goal?

Step #3: Releasing the Desperation for the Goal...

Figure out what you believe achieving the goal will change about your life... and start giving those things to yourself now. Will achieving your goal make you happy? Will achieving the goal give you more energy? Whatever you think the achievement of the goal will give you, investigate other ways to get to the same end and start living in the victory of that goal now... through other means.

Step #4: Staying in the Step You're In

What immediate action can you take today that will bring you one step closer to achieving your goal? How can you put your FULL focus (putting present mind into whole action) on taking that step in this present moment? And then continue to re-ask the question as you go from one DMA (Daily Massive Action) to the next.

At the end of the day, the only person who's going to shift your level of self-belief is you. It won't be a program. It won't be a coach… And it certainly won't be achieving the goal. Many goals get achieved with a person who believes they're an imposter because they achieved the goal they deeply believe they have no right to. Don't wait to work on your self-belief. The fastest way to achieve any big goal begins with this one step: level up your self-belief. You now have the steps. If you want to go even deeper, grab Bet on You: A Guide to Building Goal Self Belief, your free guide to self-belief. Before you dive into logistics on a big goal, take care of this and see how much faster you approach achieving that.

CHAPTER 2: WHERE ARE YOUR GOALS LIVING?

If you don't sacrifice for what you want,
what you want becomes the sacrifice.
- Unknown

What are the top 10 goals of your life right now? Stop reading this book and take fifteen to twenty minutes to write those 10 goals on a piece of paper. Better yet, go to https://kassandravaughn.lpages.co/top10lifegoals/ and download the free **My Top 10 Life Goals** worksheet. Next, pull out another sheet of paper and arrange those 10 goals in order by the sequence you think they need to be achieved in- what I like to call the **order of achievement** (**HINT:** Print out 2 copies of the 'My Top 10 Life Goals' worksheet so you can use the first copy to write your top life goals in no particular order and the second copy to place goals in your chosen order of achievement).

In other words, ask yourself:
➢ In what order should my top ten goals get achieved?
➢ Which goal comes first, second, third and fourth?

Next, decide if any goals are missing. In coming up with your top ten goals, you might write them out in the order of achievement and find yourself saying "Hmm… There are other goals that really need to happen before this goal is realistically in view."

On a separate sheet of paper, write down any goals you may have missed. Add those goals to the shuffle and put them in their proper place in the order of achievement. One caveat- these other goals should be BIG goals, not small goals or milestones that will eventually fall under the other big goals you've already listed. How do you know the difference? If a goal requires a heavy lift, i.e. there are at least five smaller goals or milestones underneath this goal that you must complete in order to achieve the goal, that goal should be separate and unto itself.

For example, you might have a goal to own a farm. But, in order to purchase that farm, you'd have to change careers so A- you can work remotely from anywhere in the country and B- you make in salary at least double what you're making right now. The changing careers is its own goal because it requires the achievement of a number of smaller goals in order to get to the full career change.

Purchasing the farm will also require other goals besides the career change so, while the career change might be a pre-requisite to owning the farm, it isn't the only thing you'd have to achieve BEFORE you could buy the farm. In this way, making the career change should be a goal that's pursued and achieved BEFORE purchasing the farm. They're related but still should be considered separate goals.

Review your goal list and make sure that all the goals you've listed are listed in the order of achievement so you now have a clear picture of what major goal should have your focus next... and here's my question for you:

Does that next goal actually have your current FULL focus? Or is your time, energy, and money going to something else?

Here's another question to ask yourself: Which of your goals have a definite expiration date and is that goal (or those goals) being properly prioritized in your order of achievement?

For example, you might list getting pregnant with your own eggs and having at least two children as a top life goal. If you're currently 43 years old and you're a woman, guess what? That goal can't be slated for five or seven years from now. No matter how important the other goals seem, either you're going to give this goal your full focus now (and possibly have to do it alongside one other goal) or you need to decide that this won't be a major life goal for you and take a ca sara sara approach- what will be will be.

And here's the point of walking you through that exercise: before you can OWN your goals, you have to get a good pulse on where each of your major life goals are living... and whether they're even goals to begin with.

Far too often, people claim to have goals that actually fall into the category of intentions or wishes.

Don't get me wrong. Intentions and wishes have their place but they are NOT goals. They are the soil in which goals grow. They may even be the initial step to setting a goal but a wish, in and of itself, is not a goal. An intention, no matter how much you feel it, is NOT a goal.

By definition, a **goal** is "an objective or target that someone is trying to achieve."

Goals are the object of your focus and they have clear metrics of success so you're able to know exactly when you've reached the desired result.

One of the first things you want to ask yourself, as you move in the direction of owning your goals, is this: "What is my relationship to goal setting?" Do you love the ideation part of goals where you get to journal, write down your dreams, and set intentions… but you dislike the logistics part of creating timelines and goal metrics?

Do you live in a place where you fear clearly identifying what the goal is because, once you write it down and there are deadlines and milestones, you start to feel trapped in doing the work and, eventually, feel resentful of having the goal in the first place? Do you struggle with the idea of setting a goal that requires a clear amount of focus each week because you know that your life is crazy and unpredictable and you don't want to see yourself fall behind on progress because of circumstances beyond your control?

There are many reasons that people find themselves in goal resistance or resentment but here's the thing I'd like you to keep in mind:

Any major goal you achieve will require that you develop goal resilience along the path of achieving it.

It's easy to live in the addiction of goal setting because setting new goals is exciting. It feels good to sit in a comfy chair and dream big, create a beautiful vision board and feel the bliss of what it will feel like to have everything on that vision board in your life. There's no better feeling than closing your eyes and experiencing, in the here and now, the life you hope your goal achievement will create for you. All of that feels amazing in the moment… but **goal setting without goal follow-through leads to massive disappointment and disillusionment in the end.** It leads you to feel hopeless in pursuit of your dreams, disgruntled about the way life has turned out and afraid to set new goals because you've now created a pattern of only getting so far into the process… and not following through.

And there is also, for many, a grave concern that, although they want to be the masters of their fate, they, in fact, are not. They believe that the storms of life will come, even if they follow through on making goal progress, and shatter their dreams, spin out their ability to focus, and steal the very goals they invested so much heart and time into achieving. Yes, people are afraid that life is more powerful than they are and that this reality makes going after goals and staying the course on goals a complete waste of time… only it's not.

In the last few years, I've started to say a particular sentence a lot… and I'm not sure where I got it from but it reflects an absolute truth:

Very often, what's right and what's easy are not the same thing.

In other words, doing what's right is, oftentimes, not the easy thing to do.

And the same applies to going after and achieving your goals. Setting goals is relatively easy. In fact, it's fun to set goals. But, the fun pretty much stops there. When you now have to transition from goal setting to goal management, this is where the newness wanes, the rose-tinted glasses come off and the rolling up of your sleeves and doing the work UNTIL becomes the boring mainstay of your life for weeks, months, and years.

There's nothing about managing your way to a goal that's exciting. The excitement wore off the moment you committed to achieving the goal. So, what do you do when you realize that you have way more fun in setting goals than achieving them? What do you do when you realize that you want to achieve a goal but you lack the will or the follow through in doing all of the daily mundane steps required to get there? How do you get over needing the thrill of goal setting to keep you motivated enough to follow through on the daily tasks of making goal progress?

Here's what you do: You own your goals… Every part of them…

And you stop demanding that excitement and passion be in every part of the goal achievement journey… because it won't be there and you have to find a way to consistently make progress without it. In <u>Own It: The Only Thing That Will Change Everything in Your Life</u>, I put it like this:

"When you're in the No Turning Back Zone, you've decided, from the start, that you've decided, from the start, that you're not leaving until you win. That's it. You're going to get this done. You're going to find a way and that level of certainty allows you to rebound and come back from failure quickly."

At the end of the day, the fastest path to building **goal resilience** (i.e. the ability to do the work for as long as it takes to get to the goal) is not being clear on what the goals are; it's being committed to giving your ALL no matter how long the goal takes to achieve.

Can you do that? Perhaps not yet but keep reading. You're going to learn how to own your goals and stay the course on them UNTIL you achieve them…

CHAPTER 3: THE FOUR QUALITIES OF A GOAL

The most difficult thing is the decision to act.
The rest is merely tenacity.
- Amelia Earhart

I like to sprint through life… and the first twenty or so years of my life were very much about sprinting. I started kindergarten a year early. I graduated from high school at 16. I got married at 18. I had my first baby at 19. I finished college at 20. I had my MBA and was a professor at the age of 22.

For whatever reason, I've always had this sense of urgency about life, as if I needed to move quickly through it to get to a certain point. That could be because my mom (who raised me as a single mother) really pushed me to accelerate and move quickly. Her take was "I'm the only one you've got and you need to grow up and make it so, in case anything happens to me, you can take care of your brother." Now… my mother didn't die early and both my brother and I grew into adulthood without losing her.

But, what I've never lost is this imminent sense of needing to move quickly through life… and my first 20 years allowed for sprinting with ease. The next 20 years, however, would not… and so began my classroom in understanding what goal achievement REALLY takes because, at the end of the day, our biggest life goals will take the longest to achieve.

So let's start at the beginning.

The word **goal** is defined in many ways, including:
- ✓ "The end toward which effort is directed."
- ✓ "The object of a person's ambition or effort."
- ✓ "An idea of the future or desired result that a person or a group of people envision, plan and commit to achieve."

What's interesting about each of the above definitions is how unhelpful those definitions are when it comes to understanding how to actually achieve any goal. I wanted to add both breadth and depth to the goal definition in this chapter by discussing the four qualities of a goal. Once you understand these qualities, you'll have a much better grasp of what it takes to set a solid goal in any area of your life.

Goals are not just about the end results you want to achieve. For a goal to serve as a blueprint for success, there are four qualities that have to be embedded within the goals you create:

- ✓ **Quality #1:** Goal Length
- ✓ **Quality #2:** Goal Breadth
- ✓ **Quality #3:** Goal Depth
- ✓ **Quality #4:** Goal Type

Goal Length

To effectively set a goal, one of the first things you need to understand about your goal is its goal length. A goal can be short or long-term. A short-term goal is a goal that takes less than two years to achieve. Any goal that takes more than two years to achieve would be considered a long-term goal. Now… I can hear people responding with "Say what???? How is a goal that takes a year and a half to achieve a short-term goal?" And here's my response: "In the grand scheme of how long it takes to achieve most big goals, anything less than two years is a very short amount of time."

Let's walk through some examples…

A college degree takes anywhere from 2 to 4 years to earn. Building and growing muscle to a point where you're lean, have a six pack, and your glutes are amazing (at least for women) typically takes 2 to 3 years to achieve. Raising your credit score from 500 to 700 can take 2 to 4 years to accomplish. Saving 20% for a down payment on a house can take a year to five years to build up, depending on how much money that is.

Paying off debt can take five or more years if you've got over $100,000 in debt (rest assured, it doesn't take very long to get into debt but quadruple the amount of time to get out of it). Dating until you meet your soulmate could take seven years. Going through infertility and hopefully getting pregnant has taken some people 8 to 10 years. Recovering your health after a major illness can take over a decade.

Changing careers when you have to go back to school in order to do so can take three to fifteen years. Becoming a doctor takes twelve years (four years of college, four years of medical school, and four years of residency). Completing a PhD program can take five to seven years. Starting and growing a business to a high six to seven figure annual revenue point can take anywhere from five to ten years.

You get my drift… and there is no such thing as overnight success. In The Year of You, I say the following:

"Reinventing yourself is going to take a lot of time, energy, and effort. I wish I could tell you that you can do reinvention in four hours a week. That's not how it works. Not only will reinvention require a ton of time every single week but it will require persistence and consistency for a very long period of time to both create the reinvention and build the lifestyle and habits necessary to sustain it."

So when you're considering the goals you want to set, it's important to first put them in the short or long-term bucket. Ask yourself "Will this goal take me less than two years to achieve… or will this goal require a longer-term investment of time, energy and money?"

And here's why putting your goals in the right bucket is a game changer. One of the keys to goal achievement comes in the form of creating and sustaining momentum. When we set goals unrealistically, we cut momentum short with the level of frustration, disappointment and discouragement that comes when we miss a goal deadline because we labeled something as short-term that, in all actuality, needed to be put in the long-term bucket.

I'll give you an example.

I got pregnant easily and unexpectedly at 18 years old and had my first child at 19. I wasn't at all ready to have a baby but I did what was required to provide for my child. A few years later, when I'd finished my MBA, was a professor, bought a nice house, had a mini-van and a puppy, I assumed that getting pregnant would once again be easy. I even decorated a nursery and redid hardwood floors because, in my mind, the 'goal' of having another baby at the age of 22 should've been a wham/bam/thank you ma'am kind of thing, right? Wrong. It took me four years of secondary infertility before I finally got pregnant with my second baby. I talk about that journey in <u>Conceiving By Faith</u>.

Now… could I have predicted how long getting pregnant and having a second baby would take? No. But, would I have felt less depression, discouragement, and sadness had I identified the goal of having another baby as a long-term goal rather than a short-term goal? You better believe I would've… and that manifested itself when I went on to try for my third baby.

Because I'd gone through four years of secondary infertility to have Baby #2, I took a much longer view on my goal of Baby #3. I said to myself "This could take four years to happen" and wasn't overly invested in getting pregnant fast. I figured "I'll try and see what happens. I'll do my best and it could take another four years to get there." And, as life so interestingly goes, after two months of trying, I was pregnant with my second baby. What do they say? If you want to see God laugh, develop a plan.

But, here's the point- my second experience of pursuing pregnancy and having another baby was so much better than my first because I'd put my goal in the appropriate bucket. I saw it as a long-term goal because, in all likelihood, it could've taken longer than two years. That didn't make me less vigilant about the DMA (Daily Massive Actions) I needed to take to improve my fertility. That didn't make me less motivated to get pregnant with Baby #2. But, what it did do for me is relieve the pressure and possible heartache that comes with going for a goal that, in all likelihood, would not be able to be achieved in a shorter timeframe.

I'm about to embark upon one of my lifelong dreams- earning my PhD in clinical psychology. Could I set the goal of getting that degree in four years? Sure. Some people do it. Would it be helpful for me to set a goal deadline that I know requires all the stars to align and everything to go just right to achieve? No, it wouldn't be helpful. Now… am I setting my goal deadline at 7 years? Certainly not. I'm holding it at 5 years but that also means this is a long-term goal and not a short-term one.

Knowing which goal length bucket your goal should live in goes a long way in helping you properly pace your consistent daily actions, keep your momentum high, and avoid the traps of discouragement, disillusionment, and frustration.

And let me say one other thing about goal length. In this 'put on a happy mask' digital world we live in, I see so many people trying to sell the 'Get rich quick' approach to everything, including achieving goals… and let me be clear about this. **There are no shortcuts to big goals that typically take people years to achieve.**

You will never convince me that a goal that takes ten years to achieve can be accomplished in six months. Can you cut the time on a goal in half by doing double the number of hours to get there? Possibly. But, a lot of teachers are out there selling this idea that you can, for example, make full time income doing part time hours. Eventually, once you've put in all of the extra time and work, you can do that. But, initially? No… that is not possible… and the reason people are selling this lie is because they know that most people won't buy a training, online program or product IF they were honest about how long getting to the goal is actually going to take.

Don't fall for it.

There's a reason things take the time they take. You need the time to learn, grow, develop, and get yourself ready for the goal. It's not just about getting the result. So much of goal achievement is about becoming the version of you who not only can achieve the result but SUSTAIN it… and that kind of personal development and growth takes time. It's not an overnight thing so don't buy into the lies people will try to tell you about how you can completely bypass the time it takes to get to big goals. You will not cheat the time mastery takes. No one will…

Goal Breadth

Breadth is defined as "wide range or extent." In this way, when I say **goal breadth**, what I mean is this: how far or wide the goal you're setting extends in your life. Meaning... some of your goals are only about this month or this year. For example, getting your oil changed is, in terms of goal breadth, a **micro goal**. It's very short-term and, yet, it's still a goal because, to maintain the health of your vehicle, the oil's got to get changed on a regular basis.

On the other hand, if your goal is to create an animal sanctuary and live out your days in Costa Rica at the sanctuary, that's a **macro goal** because it represents a goal you want to achieve over a lifetime. It's going to take a lot of micro goals to get to the macro goal of living out the rest of your life at your animal sanctuary in Costa Rica.

Within the micro and macro goal breadth designations, there are more specific goal breadth types. For example, you might have lifetime goals which can be further broken down into decade goals. Both lifetime and decade goals are **macro goals.** It's important to know this so that, as you write out your goals, you understand that your decade goals lead to your lifetime goals but both goals represent a goal breadth that is macro in nature.

For example, my lifetime goal might be to win an Oscar for best screenplay but the current decade goal is to land my first high six-figure script deal. I recognize that there are a number of things that have to happen over the next ten years to get me that high six-figure script deal so the goal breadth of the script deal goal is macro but it's also a decade goal. The goal of winning an Oscar for best screenplay is also macro but it's a lifetime goal because I understand that it may take me many script deals to finally get to the one script that gets produced and eventually leads to an Oscar win.

In the same vein, **micro goals** can be broken down into yearly goals, monthly goals, weekly goals and daily goals. They are considered micro because they're smaller in terms of what has to be completed to achieve the goal.

Goal Depth

Goal depth seeks to answer the question "How many smaller goals will be required to get to my big goal?" It's essentially about identifying how many levels deep you would have to go in terms of effort and milestone accomplishment to get to the achievement of a particular goal. To understand the goal depth connected to the goal you want to achieve, you literally need to map out all of the **critical milestones** that would need to happen in order to achieve a specific goal.

I like to think of goal depth as being one of three types:
  - Minimal
  - Moderate
  - Maximal

If the goal requires five critical milestones or less, the goal depth is **minimal**. If the goal requires more than five but less than fifteen critical milestones, the goal depth would be considered **moderate**. If, however, the goal requires anything above fifteen critical milestones, the goal depth is **extensive**.

Minimal Goal Depth

Let me give you an example of a goal that has a **minimal goal depth**. When my middle son was learning how to ride a bicycle, I thought it was going to look like this:
  - ✓ **Milestone 1:** Buy the bike with training wheels
  - ✓ **Milestone 2:** Show him how to get on the bike
  - ✓ **Milestone 3:** Hold the handlebars and take him down the street with the bike
  - ✓ **Milestone 4:** Try taking off the training wheels and let him ride
  - ✓ **Milestone 5:** He falls and wants the training wheels back on so we put the training wheels back on
  - ✓ **Milestone 6:** He rides for a week or so with the training wheels on
  - ✓ **Milestone 7:** We try him riding the bike without the training wheels
  - ✓ **Milestone 8:** He falls down and gets back on the bike and keeps riding

✓ **Milestone 9:** He learns how to ride (and not fall) without the training wheels on

In my mind, I thought there would be at least nine or ten steps to the goal of him learning how to ride a bike. In that case, my son learning to ride a bike would have had a moderate goal depth. That is not what happened.

What happened was this:
✓ **Milestone 1:** Buy the bike with the training wheels
✓ **Milestone 2:** Show him how to ride the bike with the training wheels
✓ **Milestone 3:** He watched a YouTube video on how to ride the bike without training wheels
✓ **Milestone 4:** We took off the training wheels and he rode the bike

That was it. He watched one YouTube video and taught himself how to ride the bike without the training wheels… and didn't even fall. Strange, isn't it? I thought so…

But, clearly, the goal of my son learning how to ride a bike wound up having a minimal goal depth and not the moderate goal depth I assumed it would take.

And here's why it's important to understand your goal depth- the bigger the goal depth, the more hours you'll need to invest, on a weekly basis, in working on the goal. Also, when a goal has a maximal goal depth, that tells you that either this goal, if you want it to be a short-term goal, needs to be the ONLY goal you focus on (due to all the time you're going to have to put into getting the steps done) OR this goal is, more than likely, a long-term goal and will require a significant period of time to accomplish… which is important to know so you don't set yourself up to create a goal deadline that's unrealistic.

Moderate Goal Depth
As stated earlier, if the goal requires more than five but less than twenty critical milestones, the goal depth is considered moderate. Let me give you

an example of a goal that has a moderate goal depth associated with it: improving your FICO (or credit) score.

Let's say you've had a really rough past two or three years financially and you want to set a goal of increasing your credit (FICO) score from 500 (which is pretty low) to 750. I am no expert on improving credit scores but here's what I know about what determines the FICO score (from myFICO.com):

➤ 30% of the score is based on the amount of debts you owe
➤ 10% is based on new credit you've obtained recently (I'm not sure if recently is within the last 6 months or the last year)
➤ 15% is based on how long you've had any credit history
➤ 10% is based upon your credit mix (do you have a good mix of installment loans, credit cards, a car payment, a mortgage-different types of credit)
➤ 35% is based on your payment history

Here's something I also know firsthand about your credit score- you could have a fabulous credit score (700+) one day and, if one collection goes on your credit the next month (because your creditors report to the credit bureaus every month), your score could drop considerably in ONE month from 710 to 680, depending on what thing went to collections and for how much. But, I digress…

So let's say your goal is to move from 500 to 750 as a credit score. Given the factors we just went through that determine your FICO score, here are the general steps you could take to achieve the goal of a 750 score:

➤ **Milestone 1:** Pull your credit report from all 3 credit bureaus (Experian, TransUnion, Equifax)
➤ **Milestone 2:** Dispute any incorrect pieces of information on the credit report
➤ **Milestone 3:** Sign up for a paid subscription to one of the credit bureaus (ex: Experian) and schedule time, on a daily or weekly basis, to check your credit score.
➤ **Milestone 4:** Decide what credit score factors you need to focus your attention on for the next 2 years (Do you need to reduce debt? Do you need to get new credit? Do you need a longer credit

history? Do you need to take on more debt but diversify the types of debt you take on? Are all of your monthly payments being made on time?)

➤ **Milestone 5:** Develop a 12-month plan for improving your credit score
➤ **Milestone 6:** Increase your income (so you can pay down debt)
➤ **Milestone 7:** Set up payments on auto-payment so you never miss a payment and everything gets recorded as being paid on time
➤ **Milestone 8:** Apply for one or two new forms of credit (so you diversify your credit portfolio)
➤ **Milestone 9:** Pay off collection accounts over the next 6 months
➤ **Milestone 10:** Pay all debts (including the newly gained credit) on time for 12 consecutive months

And, even in doing all of this, it may take longer to get to 750. You might actually need all collections paid off, all payments made on time, and an increased reduction of debt followed by an additional 12 months of on time payments (so 2- or 3-years total) to get to 750. The FICO score is super unpredictable- yes, you know what determines it but you never really know for sure how long it's going to take to get to a certain place.

As you can see in this example, there are ten critical milestones which puts this credit score goal at a moderate goal depth. Also keep in mind that, while some of the initial steps to this goal will take a number of hours to complete, once you put things on auto-pilot or schedule them (like checking your FICO score regularly and setting up bills on auto-payment), not much time will have to be invested (other than working and making more money) into making progress on this goal.

Also notice an interesting thing about goals with moderate goal depths- the moderate goal depth doesn't mean that the goal length won't be long-term. It could take one person two years to get their FICO score from 500 to 750 while it takes another person four years to get to the same FICO score. For the person for whom it takes four years to get to a FICO of 750, that would be a goal length that's considered long-term... and here's the thing to remember- Minimal goal depths, in most cases, tend to be short-term goals and maximal goal depths, in most cases, tend to be long-term goals but moderate goal depths can go in either direction (short- or long-term). That's important to know because many will think that the goal depth will, with 100% certainty, point to the goal length. Not necessarily so….

Maximal Goal Depth

If the goal requires anything above fifteen critical milestones, the goal depth is maximal. In most cases, a goal with over fifteen critical milestones is going to be a long-term goal. Let's go through an example.

Let's say you have a goal of building your dream home- a 5,000 square foot home on 5 acres of land in a suburb or rural area close to where you currently live. You don't have a house plan and haven't bought the land yet and you also know that you will need to double your current salary in order to afford the mortgage that will be associated with this beautiful 5,000 square foot home. Because of this, you're also aware that this is going to be a long-term goal because you feel like it'll take you 5-7 years to achieve this goal.

Let's break down the critical milestones that could lead you to this goal (Remember: There are at least a thousand ways to get to any one goal achieved. What I'm presenting here is simply one way to go about getting there. There are many other ways to do this):

> **Milestone 1:** Pull your credit report to verify that your credit score is in mortgage approval worthy range.
> **Milestone 2:** Decide what work needs to be done on your credit score and develop a plan.
> **Milestone 3:** Look at a bunch of house plans and pick out your top three. Narrow down to your #1 house plan.
> **Milestone 4:** Purchase the house plan.
> **Milestone 5:** Come up with a ballpark cost for how much the land and the mortgage on the newly built house will cost you. Use mortgage calculators to determine what that monthly payment is going to look like as well as how much you'd need to earn (in salary or business revenue) to qualify for that mortgage.
> **Milestone 6:** Reach out to at least 10 general contractors and get bids on how much they would charge to build your house plan;

also find out how booked out each contractor is and when they'd be able to build your house.

➤ **Milestone 7:** Figure out what your down payment and closing costs would need to be for the price of house you want to build.

➤ **Milestone 8:** Analyze the real estate market in the area where you'd like to build and set up alerts for land in that area so you can spend the next six to twelve months watching the market and identifying trends in price and availability

➤ **Milestone 9:** Assess the job market for your field and decide the best approach for doubling your salary or increasing revenue if you're a business owner (Is it find a better paying job in your current field, getting another degree and going for a promotion at your current place of employment, getting another degree and/or certifications and changing careers, going back to school to go into a completely different profession whose starting salaries are double what you're currently making, starting a business so you're making the money you need to make to build the house, etc.?)

➤ **Milestone 10:** Apply for jobs, certifications, or degree programs that will help you double your salary. If you're a business owner, develop the plan to double revenue in the next 1-2 years in your business.

➤ **Milestone 11:** Start the training/degree programs and/or implement the new business marketing and sales strategies.

➤ **Milestone 12:** Create a budget and savings plan that can be used to save money at your current income level and includes your savings expectations once you've doubled your salary. The savings plan should extend until the point where you have the amount of money needed for your down payment and closing costs.

➤ **Milestone 13:** Finish the additional training, college, grad school, or other skills-enhancing experiences required to increase salary or business revenue.

➤ **Milestone 14:** Apply for new jobs or grow your business' revenue and get to the income/revenue level required to qualify for building the home. NOTE: This one milestone could take years to complete.

➤ **Milestone 15:** Start the new position and/or assess the effectiveness of the business marketing and sales strategies.

- ➢ **Milestone 16:** Go for a promotion or find a new position to further increase income or change the business marketing/sales strategies to further increase business revenue.
- ➢ **Milestone 17:** Save enough money to purchase the 5-acre parcel of land.
- ➢ **Milestone 18:** Apply for and get approved for the construction loan.
- ➢ **Milestone 19:** Select the general contractor you're going to use and get on the contractor's waiting list.
- ➢ **Milestone 20:** Have the house built. It could take anywhere from 6 to twelve months to complete the home building process.
- ➢ **Milestone 21:** Finish final approvals for the mortgage and close on the house.
- ➢ **Milestone 22:** Move into your dream home.

I could keep going with milestones but, if you're feeling as overwhelmed as I am right now, there's absolutely no need to continue down this rabbit hole. Bottom line: Getting your life (and your wallet) to the place where you build your dream home will take A LOT if you're not already at the income level that would be required to qualify for and afford your dream home. In that scenario, this goal would have a maximal goal depth and would take a number of years to accomplish from start to finish. There's no shortcutting the time in this scenario.

Now… if you were the child of a wealthy tycoon who was willing to build you the house as a birthday gift, would the timeframe be much shorter? Of course. But, for many of us, that is not our reality. Knowing your goal depth sets you up for having realistic expectations about how long achieving your biggest goals will take… and this is not meant to discourage you from going after the goal.

To the contrary, getting real with what a goal requires is a way of firming up your commitment to staying the course on that goal NO MATTER how long it takes. In this way, you're not blindsided by your building of a dream home taking 7 years. You've assessed goal length, goal breadth, and goal depth and you start out the journey saying to yourself "This is going to take a long time and I'm okay with that." That level of radical acceptance puts you in a 'stay the course mindset' which is the #1 factor that will decide whether you overcome every obstacle… OR… give up at the first sign of difficulty.

Goal Type

Most people are familiar with goal types. Many books talk about a lot of different goal types. For the sake of not wanting to overwhelm you any more than I already have in this chapter, I'm going to focus our attention on six goal types:

- ➢ Type 1: Health and Fitness Goals
- ➢ Type 2: Professional Goals
- ➢ Type 3: Financial Goals
- ➢ Type 4: Relationship Goals
- ➢ Type 5: Family Goals
- ➢ Type 6: Personal Development Goals

Let's talk about each goal type…

Goal Type 1: Health and Fitness Goals

Health can be mental, physical, emotional, or psychological. When we set health goals, we're setting goals targeted at improving some aspect of our health. Self-love and self-care goals would also be included under health goals because they tie into mental, emotional, physical, and psychological health. Also included under health goals could be things like meditation, deep breathing, and journaling.

Nutrition goals revolve around your daily intake of food and beverages. Typically, people will set nutrition goals around things like daily water intake, subscribing to a particular way of eating (ex: Intermittent Fasting, Paleo, Keto), cutting back or cutting out alcohol, and food tracking.

Fitness goals are all about setting aims for how often and to what extent you exercise your body. From yoga to weightlifting to getting on your spin bike, your fitness goals will largely depend on what aspects of your physical health you've made a priority.

Goal Type 2: Professional Goals (Career or Business)

Your professional goals will vary, depending on whether you work for someone else or you work for yourself (i.e. business owner) and will encompass both if you do both (a day job and a business you're starting on the side). Professional goals are all about the objectives you have for rising through the ranks in your career or building your business revenue to a certain level. Your professional goals may include educational goals such as getting additional training, certifications, or degrees. Your professional goals, if you're a business owner, may also include things like an increase in the number of employees you have, expansion into new regions of doing business, and perhaps selling your company at a certain price point in the near future. The professional goals you set will typically require a number of critical milestones so it's important to really laser in on which professional goals feel like a MUST accomplish for you.

Goal Type 3: Financial Goals

Financial goals are targets you said that relate to things like savings, debt freedom, buying a home, investments, improving your credit score, and generating a certain amount of monthly income and/or revenue. Financial goals are deeply tied to professional goals as one will lead to (or detract from) the other.

Goal Type 4: Relationship Goals (Self, Friendship, Romantic)

Relationship goals live in the realm of how you connect to yourself and others. This is one of the most neglected goal types, partly because most people think that relationships (especially to Self) should evolve, grow, and expand with very little investment of time and effort. So not true… Setting up relationship goals around things like date nights, girlfriend getaways, doing couples counseling, taking yourself on an annual Self-Love retreat, and spending dedicated time alone going on an artist's date with yourself- all of those are examples of relationship goals. As with all other goals, it's important to quantify what success looks like in this arena. It's not enough to say "I want a better relationship with my kids." What does that actually look like every day? How would you tangibly know you achieved that? What are the metrics of relationship success with your kids? While it sounds cold and impersonal, having data points for your goal success is critical to your ability to shift strategy and change course when what you're doing isn't working.

Goal Type 5: Family Goals

Very often, family goals are lumped into relationship goals because family is all about relationships. Here's why I'm separating them- there are MANY other deep-seated issues connected to working on your relationship with family that require its own goal type. Whether the goal is to set healthy boundaries with certain family members, work on forgiveness of other family members, or rebuild relationships with your adult children, family goals are MASSIVELY complicated and require a lot of forgiveness and healing work.

Goal Type 6: Personal Development Goals

Personal development goals are goals related to the objectives you set for your own personal growth and improvement. These goals can overlap with Self Relationship Goals in that much of personal development revolves around knowing yourself, caring for yourself, and approving of yourself on a deeper level. You might set a personal development goal of reading one self-help book a week. You might also set a personal development goal of attending one conference or retreat a year. You might want to work on your suppression of emotion and make it a personal development goal to go to 1:1 therapy at least twice a month. There are many personal development goals you can set and all of them are about helping you become the best version of you.

As we conclude this chapter, I want to come back to the WHY of going over the four qualities of a goal (goal length, goal breadth, goal depth, and goal type). Far too often, when we set goals, we don't consider the key factors that will lead to us successfully accomplishing our goals by the deadlines we set.

We decide on a goal and create this arbitrary deadline without really sitting with whether the goal is a short or long term (goal length), macro or micro (is this goal a lifetime achievement goal or something I want to get done in the next year- goal breadth), maximal, moderate, or minimal (i.e., goal depth- how many critical milestones will I have to complete in order to achieve this goal?), or is in the realm of goal type that is most important to us at this season of life (i.e. is family the most important thing? Is professional the focus? Are relationships where your goal attention needs to be right now?)… and then wonder why it feels like we're failing consistently at achieving the goals we set.

When you don't set goals actively, you fail at achieving them seemingly arbitrarily… but there's nothing arbitrary about not hitting a target you didn't intentionally set. At the heart of consistent goal achievement is the ability to take both an eagle's eye view and a pigeon's perspective. You have to be able to see the bigger picture while also navigating the ground level tactical work that has to get done to achieve the vision. It'll feel like walking a tightrope but it can be done.

And it's sad that most people don't learn the intricacies of EFFECTIVE goal setting and goal management until they're in their 30s, 40s, and beyond. We're going to end that late level education right now. Keep reading AND applying what you learn in this book. Let's continue…

CHAPTER 4: THE FIRST RULE OF SUCCESSFUL GOAL SETTING

Settling is the art of taking the easy way out. Sure, it will work but you will never know what was truly in store for you if you had the courage to do what was right in your heart.
- Unknown

This morning, I withdrew from my online Master's in Social Work program. This is something I'd been working to start for nearly two years. It's a step on the journey to my goal of becoming a licensed clinical psychologist and, this morning, I typed and sent the email in three minutes flat… because withdrawing from this program was the right thing to do.

You see, I couldn't figure out why I'd been feeling so much reservation about starting this specific program. For the last two months, there was not an excited bone in my body for this program. In the last few days, as I attended the online orientation session, I kept getting this feeling of "This is not the right thing. This is not the right time. This isn't it" and I pushed it away all week because, in my logical mind, this WAS the next step. I want to get a PhD in clinical psychology. I need a therapy related degree to establish my academic ability to get into a PhD program. It makes sense.

And, yet, everything in me was saying "Not it. Not it. Not it…" So I woke up this morning and my intuition spoke clearly "Go do some research on other online MSW programs" and that's what I did… and, funny enough, I came back to the first online MSW program I'd shown interest in a few years ago and something in that program called to me yet again… But, I'd dismissed that program because it was nearly four times the cost of the program I enrolled in. In my mind, it made sense to choose the cheapest school… until this morning.

For some reason, I hadn't read the fine print about the school I was enrolled at and, this morning, the fine print screamed for my attention. It turns out the school I was about go to for my Master's in Social Work is a 3-year (part time) program and the program I originally wanted to do (that was much more expensive) could be completed in as little as sixteen months and here's where the epiphany came to me:

I settled for the wrong program when, all along, I should've simply trusted and gone with the program that was RIGHT FOR ME...

And here's what I want you to know about goal setting. The first rule of successful goal setting is a simple (but not easy) law of life:

Never settle.

And the problem with saying "Never settle" is this- Most of the time, we don't know that we're doing it... until we've already been in settling mode for a long time.

All this time, I didn't think I was settling for that online Master's in Social Work program... and, yet, I was. I was settling for less and I kept rationalizing it by focusing on the financial win it would be to earn the degree at a cheaper per semester cost. But, even that wasn't true. Three years at a cheaper price is still more money spent than sixteen months at a higher tuition rate... and even if it wasn't, here's the thing: I deserve to have the educational experience I want and I am equipped to create ways to pay for that IF I choose to.

And here's why the first rule of successful goal setting is **Never settle:** If you are settling for less, you are setting lesser goals. Period.

I put it on full blast in <u>Stop Waiting For Permission: 42 Ways to Be the Powerful Creator of Your Best Life</u> by saying the following:

"At the end of the day, playing small boils down to accepting less- from others, from life, from yourself- which then leads to waiting for other people to feed you breadcrumbs in life that, in fact, still keep you starving. Any time you accept less than you deserve, you're telling the Universe that you aren't ready for me. No one is going to disagree with giving you less if that's the standard you allow..."

And here's the point- You know you're settling by the way it feels. It feels like you're compromising your values. It feels like you're not being true to yourself. It feels like you're accepting less than you deserve... and you're feeling an undercurrent of resentment and bitterness because of it.

Notice when you feel that way and then stop yourself and ask one question: Is settling what I am CHOOSING to do? If the answer is 'Yes', keep settling. But, if the answer is 'Hell No!', in that very moment you need to make an unequivocal decision to **stop settling.**

Now... I could give you all the hows, whats and whys of doing it but deciding to no longer settle and then following through by measuring every decision against the answer to the question "Is this worthy of me?" is a very simple, straightforward process that works WHEN you unequivocally decide and do. Don't wait to make that decision. The cost of settling is way too high. Until you stop settling, any goal you set will have that weak, cowering, lukewarm feeling to it. Don't do that.

Decide that you, by nature, don't settle. The word 'settle' is not even in your mental dictionary. Set high standards. Live those standards by NOT accepting anything less... ever... and repeat, repeat, repeat... You'll get better with consistent practice. Decide and then do...

CHAPTER 5: THE FIVE PILLARS OF GOAL ACHIEVEMENT

Whatever you must do today,
do it with the confidence of a 4-year-old in a Batman cape.
- **Unknown**

I am writing this chapter a few weeks away from my 45th birthday… and there's a part of me that feels much more uncertain about what it takes to achieve a goal than I ever felt in my 20s… and maybe it's because, in my 20s, I felt absolutely unstoppable… annoyingly naïve and incredibly arrogant as I find that many 20-somethings can be.

In my 20s, I felt like I could climb Mount Everest without ever having to calculate the risk or estimate the journey and, as I've grown older, I've also grown wiser. I've witnessed myself and I spend more and more time looking at who I REALLY am and assessing if that's the person I still want to be. I do a lot more of being the observer of myself than I did in my 20s… which makes looking at goal achievement a wonky and interesting experience.

In my 20s, I thought goal achievement consisted of a 4-step process:
- I want this.
- I make a plan.
- I follow the steps and jump through the hoops.
- I get what I want.

In my 30s, I learned through a lot of trial and tribulation that I could have the best laid plans and life could then show up and, like a hurricane, completely dismantle my approach. My 30s also taught me what it means to STAY THE COURSE… even when life storms hit.

So I find myself in my 40s, with even bigger goals than I had in my 20s and 30s, sitting back and saying to myself "Okay, I don't have time to play. What's the fastest way to get there?" Truth be told, I asked that same question at 16 but, in my 40s, it takes on a much more time critical perspective.

I'm almost halfway through my life so, when I look at my goals today, I have to balance goal achievement with present moment fulfillment. When I was 20, I was racing to get my entire life to a certain point so I could enjoy that life. Now that I'm about to be 45, I find myself saying "This could be over at any minute so I need to savor today even while I'm still working my ass off to get to the tomorrow I want."

And here's where I'm going with this...

This book is designed to give you a blueprint for goal achievement and success. We spent last chapter talking about the first rule of successful goal setting. We're going to spend this chapter talking about the five pillars of goal achievement. But, let me be clear about something- I am not writing this book because I want you to put on your 20-year old mindset of "Oh, here's the plan and all I have to do is follow it and it's done." No... While the Universe DOES conspire in our favor, very often, that 'conspiring' can look like a shit storm.

The point of this book is not to teach you the step-by-step methods to GUARANTEE you achieve your goals on time. The purpose of this book is to give you a solid foundation on how to create, follow through on, and manage your goals to achievement... NO MATTER what life storms show up, what life hurricanes come to completely derail you and no matter how much YOU get in your own way... because you will.

I'm not here to tell you that everything about your goals are going to go according to plan; they are not. I'm here to teach you the methods by which you can ensure that, no matter what life throws your way, you will not give up, you will not give in, and you will not let go of what you truly want for your life, not for any reason and not under any circumstances. It is for your increased endurance, persistence, and grit that I write this book.

Know that life will challenge you. Know that the life storms will forever change you. Know that this will be hard as hell, no matter what goal you're working on... and KNOW that you are worth all the blood, sweat and tears it's going to take you to WIN. The winning, when you know how to set and manage goals effectively, now becomes inevitable. The timing will always be up for grabs. The actual crossing of the finish line becomes a certainty when you take what I'm teaching in this book and you actually LIVE it.

And my point is this- don't look for a recipe for goal success. Use this book to craft your own personalized goal achievement system so, when life tries to rock you, you have a system that YOU built to stand on... and persist.

Okay... so now that I've gotten all of that out of the way, let's focus on this chapter's topic- **the five pillars of goal achievement.**

What does it take to achieve any goal? Typically, there are 5 ingredients (or pillars) to goal success and here they are:

- ✓ Pillar #1: Goal Clarity
- ✓ Pillar #2: Goal Setting Approach
- ✓ Pillar #3: Priority Management
- ✓ Pillar #4: Habit Formation
- ✓ Pillar #5: Progress Tracking

In order to efficiently and successfully achieve a goal, all five pillars must be in place. Let's take a closer look at each one.

Pillar #1: Goal Clarity

In a nutshell, goal clarity is knowing what you want and why you want it. In describing his Law of Clarity, Brian Tracy indicates that "clarity accounts for probably 80% of success and happiness." When you are clear on what you want, clear on what it will take to get it, and especially clear on what it will take to KEEP it, you take on a level of commitment to the goal that goes beyond achieving it. Goal clarity is understanding the full life requirement of your goal BEFORE you even set the goal... so you know what you're signing up for and you're committing to being ALL IN over the lifetime of that goal.

It's about asking and answering the following questions:
1. What do I REALLY want?
2. Why do I REALLY want that?
3. How will my life change once I achieve that?
4. What will achieving that require of me and for how long?
5. What will I have to give up, shift, or put on the backburner in order to go for this goal? How willing am I to do that?
6. If it were to take 5-10 years LONGER to achieve this goal, would I still be willing to pursue it? Why or why not?
7. If I got to the end of my life and this goal wasn't achieved, how would I feel?
8. What's going to prevent me from giving up on this goal?
9. What people, situations, or dynamics could become obstacles to achieving this goal? What will I do to proactively manage those obstacles?

Question #1: What do I REALLY want?

I began Chapter 1 asking a very important question:

What are the top 10 goals of your life right now?

I'd like you to pull those goals out and, for each of the goals you listed, ask yourself the following questions:
- Where did this goal originate from?
- How much is this goal what I actually want? And how much of this goal is what someone else wants (or wanted) for me?
- What other life goals would I be willing to give up to achieve this one?

Really sit with the above questions for EACH of your ten goals. It'll take you approximately 2 to 4 hours to have enough time and space to answer the three questions for all 10 goals.

What you're going to discover, in going deep on your goals, is this: Either the ten goals you set are YOUR goals... or they're not... and, at the end of the day, the ONLY goals you'll do whatever it takes to achieve will be the goals that YOU yourself REALLY want. No matter how important you might think (consciously or unconsciously) it is to please other people, you will never stay the course on or make the level of sacrifices required to achieve a goal that isn't truly your own. Spending any length of time on goals that are not yours will lead to a lot of disappointment and heartache in the long run. Don't do it...

Question #2: Why do I REALLY want that?

Once you've gotten clear on what goals are truly YOURS, it's time to ask an equally important question: Why do I REALLY want this goal? If your goal is to earn $250,000/year, why? Why does that $250,000/year matter to you? What will it change in your life? What will it give you the ability to do? And ask the 'why' question several times. If your answer is "I want to make $250,000 in the next 12 months because I want to pay off all of my debt", then the next question is "WHY do you want to pay off all of your debt?" And you might say "Because I'm sick and tired of having debt collectors call me and feeling overwhelmed by everything I owe." Ask the question again: "Why are you sick and tired of having debt collectors call you and why are you feeling overwhelmed by everything that you owe?" and you might respond with "I'm sick of all the debt because I don't feel free. I feel stuck and I feel like a loser and I never want to feel that way again." And we might ask the question "Why do you never want to feel stuck and like a loser again?" And you might say "Because I know I'm better than that and because I know the stress of all the debt is slowly killing me and I want to live a high-quality life... and this isn't it."

So... at the end of the day, the REAL reason you want to earn $250,000/year is because you want to never feel stuck, like a loser, and as if you're slowing dying again and you know that the key to living a high-quality life comes in paying off all the debt that's keeping you feeling stuck in your own life. Do you see how much more powerful that is than the WHY of "I want to pay off all my debt"? There's no emotional zing to that first answer. So you have to do three, four, or five levels deep on the WHY to get to the REAL reason you want the goal... and that's the reason you need to bring to you remembrance whenever you feel like giving up on the goal.

Question #3: How will my life change once I achieve that?

Here's where you get to practice the art and science of envisioning your Future Self (a key component of goal achievement). Imagine and sit with how your life will look and feel different once you achieve the goal. There's nothing more disappointing in life than to spend years wanting something, finally getting it, and experiencing the reality that this thing you wanted so bad, that you toiled long and hard for, actually didn't make much of a difference to your quality of life. What a disappointment!

To avoid that level of disillusionment, take the time to imagine and sit with how your life will look and feel different once you achieve the goal. One of the best ways to do this comes in asking what, in solution focused coaching, is a technique called the **miracle question.**

And here's how the miracle question works. You say to yourself:

"Imagine that it's a normal day and you go to sleep at your normal time. Unknown to you, during the night, something happens- a miracle. Your biggest goal, the one you want the most, overnight, miraculously, got achieved. When you wake up the next morning, you can feel that something exciting has happened. Your biggest life goal has been achieved and you are now living that life. How would you know the miracle of achieving that goal happened? What would be different about your life? What would others notice about you that would signal that the goal got achieved? How would you live this day and how is that different from the day before when the goal hadn't been achieved? What would others see in your life and in you that was very different from the day before?"

It's best to journal your answers to the above questions... and what you'll start to get crystal clear on is this- the impact you expect the achievement of this goal to make on your entire life. That's a crucial piece of goal clarity.

Until you can viscerally feel the expected impact of a goal, you aren't completely sold on doing everything required to achieve it. Read that again...

In the hard times, when you feel like giving up on a goal, when it seems as if everything in your outer world is working against your efforts, being able to come back to that feeling of impact is crucial to staying the course. In many instances, being able to close your eyes and see the life your Future Self is living is one of few things that will keep you in the game of goal achievement long enough to get to that life… And it takes practice to be able to call up the vision, the images, and the feelings of what it looks like to be the person living in that future state where the goal is achieved and your life is different. Seeing and feeling your future is like building muscle- it takes repetition and practice to be able to do that in any given moment that you need the feeling. You can get there and you can call up that miraculous future. But, it begins by having a clear idea of what that future looks and feels like once the goal has been achieved.

Question #4: What will achieving that require of me and for how long?

Let me clear the air on this for all of my fellow overachieving recovering perfectionists- you will NEVER get the answer to this question right. That's not the point. In fact, for our biggest goals, it will oftentimes take MUCH longer and a lot more effort than we ever imagined it would take at the onset… and there's a reason why that's so. For many of us, if we knew that a goal we initially thought would take 2 years to achieve would actually take 12, we'd probably have switched the goal. So, it's critical that we don't know, in the beginning, with absolute certainty how long a big goal is going to take to achieve. However, we still need a ballpark deadline and amount of work so we can make the initial commitment that says "Yes, I'm willing to do that level of work for that amount of time."

Question #4 is about you getting clear on what you think the scope of work will be for your goal. Some goals are easier to figure this out for than others. If your goal is to complete a master's degree, that's pretty well laid out. If your goal is to lose weight, you can play it conservative and go with losing 1 to 2 pounds a week and have a pretty solid idea.

When we get to goals like "Meeting and marrying the love of my life", well, there's no way to know for sure how long that's going to take… and, yet, you can still have a pretty good idea of the level of effort you're going to make to achieve that goal in three to five years. Can you guarantee that you'll meet and marry the love of your life in 3-5 years? No.

You also can't guarantee that life won't kick you in the pants and your two-year grad degree morphs into a four-year part time grad experience. You don't know… and here's the thing- you still need to give yourself an initial take on what you think this goal will require of you and for how long BECAUSE you need to make a formal commitment to yourself to be ALL IN on the goal for AT LEAST that amount of effort and time. It's a way of building in accountability to doing the work of achieving your goal for a certain period of time.

Question #5: What will I have to give up, shift, or put on the backburner in order to go for this goal? How willing am I to do that?

Question #5 is one that many people shy away from answering at the outset of a goal journey… and it's something you need to make yourself respond to. Achieving goals is as much about the goals you DON'T achieve as it is about the goals you DO find victory in. In coaching, we say "Every Yes is a No and every No is a Yes." And here's what, as coaches, we mean- When you are devoting your time, energy and money to one thing, in that moment, you are not devoting your time, energy and money to another thing.

There is no being in two places at once, focusing on taking DMA (Daily Massive Action) on two goals simultaneously. The reality of life is this: All of life is about choosing and deciding to not pursue one path in favor of going the other. So you have to decide what you're willing to give up, shift, or put on the backburner in order to achieve a specific goal.

If you have a weight loss goal, maybe what you have to give up is one hour of sleep a night so you can wake up an hour earlier to fit in a 45-minute workout in your day. You're giving up an hour of sleep to work on that weight loss goal. If you have a goal of making more money, maybe you now have to add 20 hours a week of work time to your life so you can spend your normal 40 hours a week working for someone else but an additional 20 hours a week building your side hustle. Again, you're giving up everything you used to spend those extra 20 hours on each week (Netflix, family time, social gatherings, etc.) to build your side hustle.

It's critical that you evaluate what you'd be giving up, shifting or putting on the backburner so you decrease or eliminate feelings of frustration, resentment, and guilt when, in the midst of pursuing a goal, you realize just how much you've had to give up in order to do that. When you acknowledge and accept the sacrifice in the beginning, you don't feel regret in the middle or the end.

Question #6: If it were to take 5-10 years LONGER to achieve this goal, would I still be willing to pursue it? Why or why not?

This is a REALLY, REALLY important question… and here's why- you have to know if you'd still be ALL IN if you knew your goal was going to take you a decade longer to achieve it. For example, if you're 32 and you want to have children of your own so you decide to pursue fertility treatments, what if you KNEW that, at 32, it would take you a decade's worth of money, time, energy AND fertility treatments to, at the age of 42, finally have your FIRST child? Would you still go down that road if that's what it would take… or would you do something different like adopt or choose to not have children or choose to spend three years saving and building up more savings BEFORE you went on that ten-year journey?

And it's not to say that it's going to actually take you ten years longer to get to the goal but you need to really consider IF you're willing to commit that much longer to the goal IF it came to that.

Far too often, people are good with pursuing a goal so long as it only takes a few months or a year to achieve. Once we start talking about a goal taking five to ten years to achieve, people start to get really antsy and become ambivalent about whether that's a goal they really want to pursue. Determine, on the front end, whether you'd be willing to stay the course on this goal if it took you a DECADE longer to go after. Decide and then go all in with a realistic sense that, while you hope the goal will happen quickly, you're okay with staying the course if it takes way longer than that.

Question #7: If I got to the end of my life and this goal wasn't achieved, how would I feel?

Question #7 is a HEAVY question to ask and answer… and it's massively important that you answer it. Life goes by so fast and, in any given moment, most of us are saying to ourselves "I just have to get through **this**" and this could be a season of life where you're working a lot or not taking care of your body or dealing with a difficult relationship. Whatever your 'this' is, it's super easy to get so caught up in the present moment heavy lifting of life that you're doing that you completely forget how short life actually is.

Asking Question #7 stops you in your tracks and forces you to face your own mortality. Especially when it comes to achieving the biggest goals of your life, you need to stop and ask yourself what I like to call the rocking chair test. If you got to 95 years old and you're sitting on your front porch in a rocking chair looking back on your life AND you didn't achieve this goal, how would you feel? Would you feel regret? Or would you feel like "Ah, it's okay that I didn't get to that goal." As soon as you ask this question, the answer will come and the answer will tell you whether the goal you want to achieve needs your first and full attention right now... or... if the goal you want to achieve actually isn't all that important in the grand scheme of your life.

Question #7 definitely becomes a wake-up call for a lot of people living on autopilot, rushing from place to place, never stopping to pause and ask "Is what I'm doing right now relevant? Does it really matter in the grand scheme of my life?" Question #7 will remind you that you don't have forever to get your life right and that you need to be VERY selective about what you give your time to, now and for the next fifty or sixty years.

Question #8: What's going to prevent me from giving up on this goal?
It doesn't matter how badly you want a goal. At some point, you're going to want to give up... and the longer the goal takes to achieve, the more times you're going to be tempted to throw in the towel. Question #8 is a great way to prepare for those giving up moments.

It's important to decide, in advance, what strategies you'll use to keep yourself from giving up on your goals. Whether that's focusing on what you want for your kids or writing out a WHY statement that you pull out and read when you feel like giving up, you're going to want to have easy go-to tactics that you can implement when you find yourself struggling to stay the course on a big goal or dream. It's also important, when asking this question, to differentiate between what it looks like to rest versus what it looks like to quit.

Sometimes, when you're giving everything you've got to a goal and you feel completely exhausted, the answer is to rest without feeling guilt about resting. Resting means taking a day or two off of DMA (Daily Massive Action) and you've got to be able to give that to yourself without this intense fear that resting for a couple of days will lead you to quitting for a lifetime. You've got to believe in yourself more than that.

Use Question #8 to create a number of strategies that will help you keep your focus on the goal, stay the course on DMA (Daily Massive Action) AND allow for breaks when you need them. In the <u>Own Your Goals Planner Pack</u>, I've provided a 'Turn Your Obstacles into Opportunities' worksheet designed to help you proactively prepare for and work through the inevitable goal achievement challenges that will come your way.

Question #9: *What people, situations, or dynamics could become obstacles to achieving this goal? What will I do to proactively manage those obstacles?*

There will be people, situations, and other dynamics that will come into your life to block the path to your goal. Do not, for a second, think that obstacles won't come. They will and they will stop progress on your goal IF you let them. It's important to pinpoint, preferably at the beginning of a goal journey, what you think some of those obstacles will be so that, when they do show up, you don't feel blindsided by them.

As human beings, we don't love change. We like certainty and predictability and, no matter how much we quote that "the only constant is change", it's amazing how when big changes occur in our lives, we feel blindsided by them and spend weeks trying to get back to 'normal' after the change. So... save yourself some lost time by not only expecting obstacles but anticipating how you'll respond to them. The more prepared you feel for the obstacles, the less you'll focus your attention on their possibility and keep your attention on doing the work of achieving your goals.

At the end of the day, the key to having goal clarity comes in knowing that the clarity isn't simply about the goal itself; it's about what it's going to take to pursue and achieve the goal... no matter what. When you're clear on that, you're able to move forward with confidence and commitment.

When it comes to goal clarity, here's something to keep in mind: when done right, goal clarity has a TON of specificity to it. For every question listed above, you've got to get down to the details of your answer. You want answers that reflect time, place, location, years, amounts, and other details that are extremely measurable and trackable.

It's one thing to set a goal of "I want to be happy." It's quite another to set a goal that says "I want to embody happiness by taking weekly 1 hour voice lessons for the next twelve months and then singing locally at least once a month following that one year of lessons followed by writing at least ten songs in Year 3 so I can pursue and secure a recording contract by Year four." Now... "I want to be happy" is not at all specific and 'happiness' differs from individual to individual. But, the person who wants to build a singing career and defines 'happiness' as being on that journey of singing could easy measure being 'happy' by the singing goals we just outlined.

Again, goal clarity is about creating a plan for getting to a certain outcome. While the plan and the timeline will certainly change as you go, being clear about what your goal is going to require and committing to it taking as long as it takes are critical to having clarity about your goal AND commitment to achieving it.

Pillar #2: Goal Setting Approach

We're going to talk about this more in Chapter 7 but it's important to understand the power of choosing a goal setting approach that works for you. There is no point in going with a goal setting approach that you don't feel totally sold on. Like anything in life, there are at least a thousand ways to do goal setting. There is no 'one right way.' So, be mindful of how you walk through life, of what resonates with you, and customize your goal setting approach to YOURSELF. If you have to create a brand-new goal setting approach, do that... and here's why: **You won't follow an approach that doesn't resonate with who you are.** You won't. It's pointless to pick up Tony Robbins' goal setting approach or Brian Tracy's goal setting method or my goal setting protocol IF it doesn't feel like the right fit for who you are and how you move through the world.

Habits are very similar in this way. You might love Charles Duhiggs' The Power of Habit approach to developing habits… or you might hate it. You might admire BJ Fogg's approach to habit building in Tiny Habits but find it cumbersome to apply to your own life. Maybe you deeply resonate with James Clear's Atomic Habits and that feels like a natural fit for you. Well, the same applies to the goal setting approach you choose.

Your goal setting approach has to feel natural to you. It's got to work with your life. For example, I like to spend a lot of time in the morning writing out my goals. I got that tip from Grant Cardone and I firmly see its value… and it takes me anywhere from 30 minutes to 2 hours to do my goal writing/reviewing process. Not every person wants to take that kind of time out of each day to do it… and I get that… and it's not for everyone but it is for me.

So here's what I'm saying: Make sure whatever goal setting approach you use IS for YOU. Just because someone else uses a particular approach successfully doesn't mean it will work as successfully in your life. At the end of the day, the goal setting approach that will work best for you is the goal setting approach you're going to use consistently… so look around, do your homework, and choose an approach that resonates so deeply that you'll do it with ease, even on the hard days. That's going to be the goal setting approach for you.

Pillar #3: Priority Management

The third pillar to goal achievement is priority management. Priority management is NOT the same thing as goal management. Priority management is the art and science of managing your priorities, both on a macro and micro level. It's about connecting your long term goals to the daily, weekly, and monthly priorities that you set. I was listening to one of my favorite podcasts this morning and the coach asked this question:

Do your actions line up with your goals?

That's an ESSENTIAL question to answer when you're doing priority management… and, far too often, people will set a big goal, really want to achieve that goal and, yet, they'll prioritize everything but the actions it will take to get to that goal in their daily and weekly schedule. That won't lead to goal achievement.

Priority management is about taking, on a daily basis, a good hard look at the time you have available to work on things and asking yourself the questions:

- ✓ What are my top three priorities for today?
- ✓ How do each of those priorities feed into making consistent progress on my goals?
- ✓ If I could only get one of those top three priorities done today, what would be my #1 thing?
- ✓ What are the next three steps to accomplishing that #1 priority today?

And it can feel like a battle of elimination because what you're essentially doing is deciding what your ONE Thing is and focusing all of your attention today on that UNTIL it's done… and then asking the question again.

Many people will see that as being super limiting. It can feel, by prioritizing, that you aren't getting that much done in a given day. Here's the reality- most people overpromise and under-deliver in their own lives. They think they have more time to get things done than they actually do… and then wonder why they end each day feeling like a failure… and it's because they set themselves up for failure by attempting to get done what could not be done that day given the amount of time they had to work on things.

And I'm not saying that it doesn't feel hard to admit to yourself how little you can actually get done in a given day. Achievement disappointment is a real thing. It's hard to look at how little can actually get done in a 24-hour period when it feels way more fulfilling to believe you can get twice as many deliverables completed.

Using magical thinking to prioritize your day will lead to a level of unrealistic expectation and disappointment that will tank your level of self-belief and self-trust. Don't do that. By committing to what you can accomplish in a given day and getting that amount of work done day after day, you're going to notice every aspect of your Self increase (self-worth, self-belief, and self-confidence).

When you set daily goals, you're going to also notice that you have no doubt about your ability to achieve the things you decide to achieve because now, you've built up the lived experience that when you say you're going to do something, it gets done... and that level of self-certainty is worth its weight in gold when it comes to goal achievement.

At this point, you might be asking yourself "Okay, so how do I do priority management?"
I've created a very simple approach to this that's included in the <u>Own Your Goals Planner Pack</u>. It's a Reverse Engineering Decade Goals worksheet where you connect your decade goals to the current year goals. By writing this down on a daily basis, you make the connection between your long-term goals and the goals you'll need to achieve this year to get closer to those decade goals. At the bottom of the worksheet is a space for you to (for each of your 3-4 decade goals) write down the 3-4 DMA (Daily Massive Actions) you're going to take today to get you closer to each of those decade goals (one DMA per decade goal).

From there, you can then decide which, of the 3-4 DMAs, are your #1 priority for today and go into immediate action for getting that first Daily Massive Action done. In my mind, that's the simplest way, on a daily basis, to prioritize tasks.

Another way to do priority management might include mapping out each of your big goals. In this case, you'd take out a sheet of paper and, at the top, write down the goal. Underneath the goal, list out all of the steps it would take to complete the goal. Once you have all the steps listed, you'd then want to pull out another sheet of paper and put all of the steps you listed on the first sheet of paper in proper sequence (what I like to call **the order of**

operations). Once you have all the steps for achieving your goal listed in order of completion, you could then assign due dates to each of those steps. Those due dates would serve as your indicator of priority because you'd now know which smaller goals needed to be accomplished next.

I sometimes use this method if I'm creating brand new goals that have not been on my decade or yearly goal list before. The only complication with using this order of operations approach to priority management is that you might discover, by mapping out three or four big goals, that the deadlines for smaller goals under each bigger goal, fall in the same time range as the micro-goals for another bigger goal... and without having an adequate gauge on how long it will take to complete each of the smaller goals within the same timeframe, you may find yourself overwhelmed, not able to complete both sets of smaller goals for both bigger goals, and stuck in a cycle of underachieving because you don't see how you can possibly accomplish all the smaller goals you have a similar deadline for.

Again, the key is this- find a priority management strategy that aligns with and works for you...

Pillar #4: Habit Formation

The achievement of any goal boils down to the habits you've created that result in consistent progress over a long period of time. In Atomic Habits, James Clear puts it like this - "Eventually, I began to realize that my results had very little to do with the goals I set and nearly everything to do with the systems I followed."

He goes on to say, "Goals are about the results you want to achieve. Systems are about the processes that lead to those results."

To achieve any big goal, you need to develop consistent approaches to how progress will be made on that goal. That is why, for example, when it comes to a weight loss goal, meal prep is key... and the system isn't just that you prep your food for a week. When you have a solid system for achieving the weight loss goal, you literally schedule two to three hours on your calendar for the same day each week to DO the meal prepping. That way, there's no second-guessing A- that meal prepping will be done and B-when it will be done. Having that system of meal prepping cuts down on the energy you might waste on deciding, each week, when and whether to meal prep. It also creates a habit around meal prepping that, after a few weeks, will become second nature to you.

As James Clear says in <u>Atomic Habits,</u> "Fix the inputs and the outputs will fix themselves."

Before we get into habit formation, it's important to address the elephant in the room- how many habits can you form at one time? And here's what I've found in my own life- I can form 2 to 3 habits MAXIMUM at the same time. Keep in mind that it takes at least 90 days of consistent habit practice before the habit neurologically goes on auto-pilot. For many goals, it takes WAY longer than 90 days to get to that place. Because it can take you months to develop that automatic sense of "This is what I do" with any one habit, trying to build more than three new habits at the same time tends to create a lot of confusion for the brain.

You might be saying to yourself "But my top 10 life goals require that I develop so many habits that I don't currently practice! Heck, even my #1 goal requires developing so many habits that I don't currently practice. How do I not work on developing all of those habits if developing those habits is key to my achieving those goals?"

And here's what I'm going to say- You have to prioritize and choose. I'm currently rebuilding a habit of writing 4,000 words/day EVERY SINGLE DAY... and I recognize that it's going to take me months to get back to a habit that, at one time, felt so simple. But, this daily writing habit matters because, if I'm going to hit my goal of publishing 52 books (this book is Book #35), I can't afford to miss a day of writing. And here's the other thing, when I don't write daily, I lose time having to reconnect with my work because I put a day or two in between my last writing session.

Now... what habit building am I having to give up by focusing on this 4,000 words/day habit? If you've read any of my other books, you know how I feel about working out in the morning. I LOVE it and, more than likely, if an early am workout doesn't happen, it typically won't. But, guess when I write best? Early in the morning. So, as I build my daily writing habit, I've had to allow my workout habit to take a backseat and I'm having to make peace with the fact that it's far more important for me to cultivate 1- the daily writing habit and 2- the meal planning/eating clean habit than it is to enforce the daily workout habit.

Why?

Because, even with my weight loss goal, having been a personal trainer years ago, I know one thing is true- 80% of weight loss is what you eat, not how hard you work out. So, while I adore my workouts and they're like therapy sessions for me, given my current priorities, it's more important that I develop the habits of writing daily and eating clean (both of which can happen simultaneously without cutting into the scheduled times for either) than it is to still hold onto the enforcement of the workout habit.

Am I still getting in workouts consistently? Yes. Are they a priority or as long as I'd like them to be? No.

And that's the first thing you have to decide about your habits- the two to three habits that you want to focus on developing now… and the other habits that you are going to intentionally leave by the wayside until these first two or three are firmly set and operating on autopilot… and there's experimentation to this. In focusing on my daily writing habit, I may find, in time, that the daily workouts are much more vital than the daily writing habit… and I may have to switch things up again. Remember that all of this, at first, is about experimenting with habits until you determine which habits are most vital FOR YOU… and then doubling down on those two to three habits for the long term.

Okay… so the first thing you have to do with habit formation is select the two to three habits that are most important for you to develop right now. What you'll find is that if you've selected the right first habits, they, more than likely, actually impact ALL of your biggest goals. For example, eating clean, as a habit, affects your energy, ability to focus, mood and psychological/physical health which, no matter what your biggest life goals are, will help you achieve those goals. The habit of eating clean is a domino habit in that, once you put that habit on autopilot, it makes achieving ALL of your goals that much easier to do.

So you select the two or three habits that you want to spend at least the next 90 days testing and developing. Now it's time to get down to tactics related to actual habit formation.

Going back to James Clear's ideas on habit formation in <u>Atomic Habits,</u> here's a simple way to approach developing any habit:
- ✓ *Step #1:* Determine the time of day when you're least likely to be disturbed, sidetracked or derailed from completing the habit
- ✓ *Step #2:* Schedule the practice of that habit on your calendar (indicate both time and location)
- ✓ *Step #3:* Try to pair this new habit with a habit you already have firmly in place (habit stacking)

Let's use my daily writing time as an example. For years at this point, I have a daily habit of waking up, giving my dog a treat, starting the kettle boiling for tea, having red raspberry leaf tea as I sit down to my computer to check email and do my daily revenue review. The having tea as I sit at my laptop doing my daily revenue review is a daily habit that, after practicing for years, is on autopilot. So… with my daily writing goal, what I've done is scheduled writing time to occur from 6 am to 9 am seven days a week (I wake up at 5 am and have my tea and revenue review done by 6 am. Built into those three hours are some down time to get up, stretch, watch a YouTube video because I know it typically takes me two hours to write 4,000 words (not three) but I have buffer time in there.

As you can see, I'm habit stacking the morning tea and revenue review with the new habit of writing 4,000 words each morning. I've also decided on writing time that happens at the same time with a three-hour focus block EVERY SINGLE DAY. It is also the case that writing at 6 am is when I am at my most creative place and no one else in my house is awake so I'm most likely to get all 4,000 words done in that timeframe without being disturbed by anyone, including my dog who simply sleeps on his doggie bed in my office.

That's a simple way to develop a new habit. For more ideas on habit development, be sure to read James Clear's book <u>Atomic Habits</u>.

Pillar #5: Progress Tracking

The fifth pillar of goal achievement is, in my coaching experience, the hardest one to get people to do... and, yet, it's the one that guarantees the fastest path to success... and it's progress tracking. I always say this:

You can't secure success for results you refuse to measure.

The buck stops with you. If I have a weight loss goal of losing two pounds a week but I absolutely refuse to get on the scale each week and/or take tape measurements on a consistent basis, then how do I expect to achieve that goal? How do I even know that I'm on track for achieving that goal? Here's the thing- I don't.

Progress tracking is a powerful tool that can help you adjust strategy as you go on your goal journey. You don't want to spend years using an effective goal strategy only to come to your goal deadline and figure out that everything you put into achieving the goal didn't work and wasn't the right approach. That's wasting months or years of your life that you'll never get back.

Progress tracking, no matter how you do it, is about having a central place where you keep track of your goal progress. I'm a big believer in using spreadsheets to stay on the pulse of daily progress. I also love spreadsheets where there's a column for notes so I can give further description to why a particular day did or didn't go as planned.

Part of my progress tracking method involves color coding my daily metrics so, if a particular metric is colored red and has an N in the box, I know it didn't get done that day. If it remains blue and has a Y in the box, I know I accomplished it. Over time, all I have to do is take a look at the overall spreadsheet and, from week to week, I can see if I'm being consistent with my DMA (Daily Massive Action).

For items that I find myself being completely inconsistent on for more than 3 weeks, I take a harder look at that metric and ask myself "Is this really necessary to me achieving the goal? If it isn't, why do I have this metric here? If it is, do I need to do different things to reinforce getting this daily metric done… or do I need to change the goal?" That kind of analysis leads to changed strategy, changed behavior, or both, all of which helps me get to my goal that much faster.

When I'm coaching clients who are afraid of tracking progress, typically the thing that comes up is this: "If I'm not consistent, I'm going to feel really bad about myself and it's going to make me not want to do anything." That could be one way to look at it but what if we did a mindset shift on that perspective? What if, instead of seeing daily metrics as persecutory illumination of your unworthiness, we looked at having a progress tracker as a source of motivation and encouragement, a way to see if what you're doing is working FOR YOU… or if there are things you'd like to and can change about your daily metrics so that you feel more inclined to be consistent and to follow through? What if the progress tracker is a way to celebrate all of the things you are doing on a daily basis rather than going from day to day saying to yourself "Are we there yet?"

You see, the progress tracker is not about labeling you a certain kind of person. It's about holding you to your own self-commitments about the kind of person you're capable of being… and it's also about not expecting perfection from the start. Typically, when I begin my progress tracker, the first few weeks (and, at times, the first few months) are awful in terms of consistency! I see so many red boxes, it sickens me. And then I start to ask myself some powerful questions, like:

- What's causing me to not get this done?
- What's getting in my way?
- How could I make this daily metric easy to do?
- Does this need to be scheduled at a different time in my daily schedule?
- Whose support do I need to get this done?
- Is this truly relevant to me accomplishing my goal… or is this a vanity metric that I put in there just because it's 'hard'?
- Do I have too many daily metrics to achieve?

☐ How can I whittle down the number of things I'm asking myself to do every day and still get things done?

☐ What's at the root of me not following through and how do I address the root cause of the issue?

Now… you're not sitting in the blame/shame/guilt vicious cycle and you're actually problem solving and looking for new possibilities that will help you be more consistent. But, if you never track your consistency, how do you know that you need that kind of intervention? You don't…

It's also helpful to incorporate celebration tactics and rewards for every week that you get all blues on your progress tracker. There's a definite dopamine hit that comes when you're able to check the boxes of achievement for seven days straight.

• How do you want to celebrate that on a weekly basis?

• What can you do to make your following through on consecutive days enticing and worth whatever work it takes?

Figure out a reward system that will keep you focused and dialed in… and then truly take the time to celebrate and reward yourself every single week as you follow through with vigilant consistency.

At the end of the day, the five pillars of goal achievement form the foundation of getting to victory lane on any goal. Having goal clarity, an aligned goal setting approach, doing priority management well, forming habits that stick, and tracking your progress daily are the five things that will decide whether you achieve your goal or never get there. Do not dismiss the power of any one pillar. They work in concert with each other and they form the foundation of the future you're now creating.

Your goal isn't to be perfect at each pillar. It's to be aware of each pillar, to understand how each pillar needs to work for your goals, and to do what is required to develop competency within each of them.

It will take time to do that. Don't rush the process but, also, don't dismiss it either. Your ability to do what each pillar requires will decide if your future will be exactly what you're hoping it will become.

Don't give up. Don't give in. Don't allow overwhelm to sidetrack you. Take this step by step and let's keep going...

CHAPTER 6: WHAT'S YOUR MINDSET ON GOAL ACHIEVEMENT?

It's not the plane. It's the pilot.
- Top Gun Maverick

Before we dive into the tactics and strategies related to goal achievement, I want to use this chapter to dive into a topic that is far more important: **your mindset.**

I want you to take a minute and think about the current goals you have in your life. Maybe you want to start a business or write a book or get physically fit. Take a few minutes and go over in your mind all the goals you would absolutely love to achieve in this season of your life.

Now... I want you to go through each of the goals you identified and both ask and answer one question:

Is the goal optional... or inevitable?

Really sit with that question. Is the goal of getting into the fittest shape of your life a wonderful possibility, a great goal to pursue, and something that you "should" do... but not something that, in this season, you feel you MUST do? The answer to that question will tell you a lot about the likelihood of achieving that particular goal... and here's where I'm going with this. If the goal you want to achieve is a 'should' and not a MUST, then you have already created a goal that has exit ramps built into it that, at some point, you're going to take.

Tony Robbins talks a lot about the difference between 'should' and 'must' and he says the following: "People don't get their 'shoulds.' They get their 'musts.'" From a mindset coaching perspective, this is the issue we need to work on BEFORE we get into goal tactics and strategies.

✓ Is the goal you're going after so *compelling* that, in your own mind, you have no choice but to go after AND achieve it?

✓ Are you so driven by the goal that you are willing to set aside whatever has to be set aside so you can give the time and attention to achieving this ONE thing?

✓ Are you ready to say 'No' to all the things you want to say 'Yes' to in favor of focusing on this goal?

✓ Are you going to push yourself outside of numerous comfort zones and not give up on the dream, even in moments when you're frustrated, exhausted, and feel like giving up?

✓ Is it so massively important that you get to this goal AS FAST AS YOU CAN that you have become obsessed with taking as many Daily Massive Actions (DMA) as you can day in and day out?

These are the questions you need to ask yourself and, yet, far too many people spend the bulk of their time focusing on the plan, the strategies and the tactics… as if improperly set logistics is the reason they haven't achieved the goal. Let's be clear- logistics matter but poor planning or a wonky goal setting system is NOT the reason you didn't achieve the goal the last time you went for it.

Pulling from Top Gun Maverick, here's the reason you didn't achieve your goal the last time you went for it:

"It's not the plane. It's the pilot."

It's you… and the truth of this is not meant to send you into a blame/shame/guilt game spiral. On the contrary, this is meant to empower you because the entire basis upon which your goal success lives has always been and will always be you… and until you can accept that it is YOUR tenacity, YOUR grit, YOUR focus, YOUR commitment, YOUR time, and YOUR energy that makes all the difference in YOUR goal attainment, you will live in the space of trying to blame your lack of goal achievement on factors, people, and situations outside of yourself, therefore turning over your power of success to those external forces.

Don't do that.

Goal achievement comes down to your mindset. It comes down to you deciding that there is no exit ramp for this goal, that you are going to do what it takes to achieve it NO MATTER HOW LONG it takes to get there. It's a mindset that can be cultivated.

And maybe you haven't yet developed a tenacious, relentless mindset. Maybe you have a history of taking every back door possible out of previous goals you set, especially when the going got tough... and here's what I want to say to that: Welcome to the club.

We've all fallen short. We've all cut out on goals when the going got tough. We've all played the victim at one time or another. All of those errors are in the past. That might have been who you WERE; that doesn't need to be who you ARE...

So, how do you shift your mindset on goal achievement from 'should' to MUST?

Here's what you do: Take a look at every limiting belief, personality defect, and disempowering thought that you have about achieving your goal and say to each and every one of them "Get the fuck out of my way." You heard me right.

We so easily want to say that to people in our lives who are sabotaging our success and, even if we don't say that to them, oftentimes, our behavior towards them will relay the message "Get the fuck out of my way." And, yet, we are not as vigilant about saying that to all the internal battles we keep repeating within ourselves that only serve to squash our dreams, steal our focus, and sabotage our success.

No... it's time for you to, moment by moment, thought by thought, get to a place that when something hits you that you KNOW isn't getting you closer to the goal, you stop everything you're doing and you say to yourself "Get the fuck out of my way."

In <u>Uncover Your REAL Fears: Face Your Fears and Move Beyond Them</u>, I used to refer to this strategy as **SDASU**- telling your fear to **Sit Down And**

Shut Up. I now see that the strategy, especially when it comes to leveling up your life and going after things you've never gone after before, needs to be much bolder and much more brazen.

You need to catch yourself in moments when you're giving 80% to the goal (and not the 100% you MUST give) and say to yourself "Umm, no ma'am. No sir. We are not half assing this process. Get the fuck out of my way."

You need to stop yourself when the self-doubt starts to rage and you begin to question if you can even achieve this goal and say to yourself "There are people with less talent, less ability, and less commitment who are out in these streets making it happen. Get the fuck out of my way."

In moments when you feel like you're doing 'all the things' and nothing seems to be moving, you need to stop yourself and say "Have I been doing this ALL IN for the last 365 days consecutively? What about the last 3 years consecutively? Stop the whining and get your butt ALL IN on the actions you need to take RIGHT NOW. Get the fuck out of my way."

And here's why having this internal conversation whenever you need to have it REALLY matters. Your biggest obstacle to goal achievement will never be anything outside of you. **Your biggest obstacle to your best life will always be YOU.**

This life is a competition between you and you... and not anyone else. Let's not pretend like it's otherwise.

So the mindset you need to build AS you learn the strategies contained in this book is a relentless mindset that calls you out on your bullshit whenever it shows up. Get good at being honest with yourself about when you're half assing a goal attempt. Be real about the moments when you are taking action in a lukewarm way because it's what you 'should' do instead of firing up your energy and getting yourself into the place of taking DMA (Daily Massive Action) because ALL IN is the ONLY way you show up to your goals.

I saw a quote the other day by Dan Koe that really points to the distinction I'm talking about and here's what Dan had to say:

"You feel bad because your Future Self is watching your every move, and they don't like what they see…"

And that's your litmus test. Whenever you are applying any of the strategies contained in this book and, yet, you're feeling like adequate progress isn't being made, stop and ask the question: "If my Future Self was watching me right now, would my Future Self like what she sees? Would my Future Self be proud of the effort I'm making? Would my Future Self see that I'm giving this goal EVERYTHING I've got? Or… would my Future Self witness me wasting time, not handling my business, putting forth half ass effort, operating in a spirit of entitlement, complaining, and playing the victim? If my Future Self were in my head right now, how would he feel about the things I keep saying to myself as I take the actions required to get to my goals?"

When you begin to assess the quality of your goal action taking through the lens of your Future Self, you start to get VERY clear about how valiant and effective your efforts actually are… or aren't.

I'm going to give you a lot of strategies for goal achievement throughout this book. But, none of those strategies will work if you aren't navigating this mindset piece well… and let me say another unpopular thing to consider: **The mindset you're capable of has A LOT to do with the foods you eat.**

I'm a former personal trainer and I've been in and out of shape. I've put my body through every extreme you can imagine and here's what I've learned in going through those things- my mindset is far easier to manage and far more powerful in its tenacity when my hormones aren't out of whack… and my hormonal balance is dictated by the foods I eat and the ways in which those foods interact with my neurochemistry.

And I'm not saying this to body shame or food shame anyone. I myself struggle with emotional eating. I myself am someone who is 0/100 when it comes to fitness and nutrition. Either I'm all the way dialed in or all the way dialed out… and I'm no longer fighting that reality. I'm not telling you eating clean is easy. It has never been easy for me.

Here's what I am telling you- I am at my best physically, mentally and emotionally when I go ALL IN on my nutrition and get it 100% dialed in. Is it fun? No. Do I crave all the yummy foods? Absolutely. But, especially as I get older, I see how the foods I eat debilitate my health in all ways… and, in my 40s, at this age and stage, I can't afford to lose any amount of time to nonsense I CAN control.

Take my advice for what it's worth but the proof is in the pudding. Here's an experiment to try so you can get a sense of how your nutrition is impacting you. Spend one week eating the way you now eat and keep a journal of how you feel after every meal. Eat a meal, wait 10-15 minutes and then journal how you feel physically and emotionally. The next week, be SUPER intentional about eating ONLY clean foods. Cut the junk and processed foods. Eat protein with every meal. Drink more water. Don't necessarily cut out caffeine because the caffeine withdrawal can last up to two weeks. Do cut out the sugar with the coffee. Jot down, after each meal, how you feel. It would be even better to do this clean eating experiment for a month.

After the month, re-read your journal entries. The proof will be there. And here's my point: When your goal has your complete and total focus, you will do EVERYTHING in your power to give it your best shot. You will control every factor related to your goal achievement that you possibly can control.

One last thing I want you to keep in mind and these are the words of Tom Bilyeu:
"I'm going to do what my goals demand."

Anthony Trucks put it another way:
"Whatever your dream is, that is the pace at which you have to go."

From a mindset perspective, we so often ask the wrong questions when it comes to achieving our goals. We ask "How much time do I have to work on this?" or "Is this possible to achieve?" Both of those questions are leading down the direction of doing the minimum because both lead to a limiting conversation that sounds something like this:

"I don't have enough time to get all of that done... There's no way I can be consistent with this for the next six months... I don't have three months to achieve this goal. It's got to happen now and, if it can't happen now, why bother? I'm already exhausted. How could I possibly add more to my plate?"

The excuses can go on forever... and here's the mindset shift I want you to make:

You have the power, the capacity, and the ability to do what your goals demand. Period. End of story. No need for excuses to be in the mix.

When you decide that you have the ability to do what your goals demand, to, as Anthony Trucks puts it "Learn to normalize and accelerate", you stop giving in to the exit ramps that show up along the way. You stop looking for all of the reasons why going for this goal will lead you to overwhelm and burnout. You stop making the excuse that your focus needs to be in every direction but your goal. You own the fact that you have massive capacity to focus on more than one thing. You own the fact that you can leverage your energy and your determination to do the hard things and get the job done. You own the fact that if you really, really want to make this happen, there is nothing in this world that can stop you. You own all of it and you move forward.

The mindset is about taking control of your goal and not letting the challenges of achieving your goal have control over you. No, that's not easy to do but it is simple to move forward with and it is a far better approach than giving all of the outside forces more power over you than you have over yourself.

Work on your mindset. Remind yourself daily that you are going to do what your goals demand... and then do that... and notice how things change...

CHAPTER 7: THE MYTH OF SMART GOALS AND OTHER GOAL SETTING TECHNIQUES

Everybody has a dream but not everybody has a grind.
- Eric Thomas

Let's start this chapter with a truth that none of us can run away from:

Goals that get achieved are goals that were set properly.

And, by set properly, I'm referring to a number of factors that we'll go over in this chapter.

When it comes to achieving goals, one of the biggest mistakes I see people and organizations making comes in the belief that having a 'solid' goal setting approach is the key to accomplishing any goal... and I see large corporations selling the idea that having a 'clearly defined goal setting approach' is the means by which great goals are created and achieved. Not true...

Your goal setting approach will mean nothing if it doesn't feel aligned to the way you walk through life. Believing that having the 'right' goal setting approach is the key to guaranteeing your goal setting success is like saying all you have to do to lose weight is select the right diet. No... the diet has to actually be the right fit for you AND THEN you have to be vigilantly consistent with the diet to see the results you're going for.

In the same way that there is no magic formula diet, there is no magic formula goal setting approach that's going to cause you to stay the course on doing the work of getting to your goal. That's not the purpose of having a goal setting approach.

The purpose of having a method by which you set goals is this:
To create a system for your goal setting that meets a common set of criteria so, over time, goal setting takes you less time to do BECAUSE you have a proven system that works.

Now… there's a lot in that purpose.

Your goal setting approach has got to make sense to you. It's got to work for you and your life. It's got to be an approach that you find at least somewhat enjoyable to participate in. It's also got to be an approach that consistently leads you to achieving those goals… and all of those criteria pieces result in what I mean when I say the goal setting approach has got to be aligned to the way you walk through life.

Here's the other thing to keep in mind: No goal setting approach results in achieved goals if you start out with setting too many goals that will take far longer to achieve than the deadlines you set up because you haven't adequately assessed the investment of time, energy, and money it will take to achieve each of the goals at the same time.

A lot of people want to blame their goal setting approach for why they didn't achieve the goal when, in fact, if they had actually taken a step back and looked at how many goals they were going for in a particular period of time AND how much time each goal would've actually required of them, they would've known, from the start, that they were sabotaging their ability to achieve ALL of the goals by starting out with too many goals to begin with. Having a solid goal setting approach won't alleviate the disaster of trying to accomplish more than you realistically can accomplish in a given period of time. But, having the right goal setting approach will go a long way in helping you avoid making that mistake in the first place.

And I get this question a lot from people:
Do I actually need a goal setting approach?

I especially get that question from those who consider themselves "free spirits" and don't want to feel tied down to any particular method for achieving their dreams… and here's my response:

EVERYONE needs a goal setting approach.

Now… your goal setting approach might be super woo-woo because you're super woo woo. It might involve crystals, chakras, sage, vision boards, and then journaling for hours. If that works for you (i.e. if the goals get accomplished when you say they will), then make that your goal setting approach and stick to it. However, goal setting is not simply about setting intentions. It's about defining all of the strategies, tactics, and deliverables that will be required to bring the intention to life.

Yes, everyone needs a goal setting approach and, yes, it's much easier to pull from a currently existing one, modify it to suit your needs, and move forward with it than it is to spend days and weeks meditating on what your personalized approach should be and then creating that from scratch… which is why we're going to spend this chapter going over the ins and outs of several already established goal setting approaches.

Before we get into each of those, I want to answer another question I get a lot:

Should the goal setting approach I use be research backed?

Once again, I see so many companies spending millions of dollars on consulting firms and companies claiming to be able to implement a 'goal setting approach' that's 'empirically backed.' Once again, here's what I'm going to say to that: **Not necessarily…**

Whether it's for a company or for an individual, I care less about whether the goal setting approach you use has decades of biased, university performed research behind it indicating that it works. I don't care if it worked for the six hundred, not-so-random participants a company or university pulled together for a six-week study. That's not reliable to me.

What I care about is whether that goal setting approach actually works FOR YOU… and you won't know that until you implement and use it for a LONG period of time… meaning not six weeks or even six months like so many studies have done. It takes a long time to figure out if the goal setting approach you're using is effective AND also if the way you're using it is effective.

Let's dismiss the idea that "research backed" means it'll work for you. Maybe it will; maybe it won't… and do not make that a requirement for you trying an approach out. All of this is an experiment. Be open to trying out-of-the box things. That's the fastest way for you to find the goal setting approach that is right for you.

Okay, so we're going to go over the following goal setting approaches:
1. SMART
2. 6 Ws
3. PACT Method
4. The ONE Thing
5. Brian Tracy's approach

Goal Setting Approach #1: SMART

One of the most well-known examples of a goal setting approach that has been taught in almost every MBA degree program for the last twenty years is the SMART goal setting method. SMART was created by George T. Doran in 1981. He was a consultant and former director of corporate planning for Washington Water Power Company. Having published a paper called "There's a SMART Way to Write Management's Goals and Objectives", Doran introduced the concept of SMART goals as a way of developing a clearly defined roadmap to accomplishing a goal.

SMART is an acronym for: **Specific, Measurable, Achievable, Relevant, and Timebound.**

For a goal to be SMART, a goal must have the following components:

Specific

For a goal to be adequately achieved, it's got to be specific. Specific means that you're laying out what the goal is, the result that signifies achieving the goal, the due date for achieving the goal and, somewhere in the description of the goal, hint at the importance (or the WHY) of the goal. A lot of what makes a goal 'specific' will be found in the other pieces of the SMART acronym (Measurable, Achievable, Relevant, and Time Bound). Having the other four components naturally leads to the goal being specific.

Let's walk through an example.

Jane's initial goal is to walk every day. Already, the goal has some level of specificity to it. But, if we were to say to Jane "Walking two minutes a day is achieving that goal. Is that what you were going for?", Jane could easily respond and say "Oh no! Two minutes a day does not satisfy what I view as achieving this goal."

Jane would then need to get more specific about what goal achievement looks like for her.

A more specific goal might look like "Getting in a minimum of 5,000 steps every single day for the next thirty days." Now we've got a walking goal that is specific, measurable (because Jane can wear a smart device that tracks her steps), achievable because Jane could probably get those 5,000 steps in through 30 minutes of walking per day and Jane's allotted 30 minutes a day for a walk, relevant because Jane's bigger goal is to increase her cardiovascular health (and walking is a good first step), and time bound. She wants to work on this goal and achieve it in the next thirty days.

Again, the walking every day had some level of specificity and measurability to it but not enough. It needed to be more specific so it could be measured with more accuracy.

Measurable

The M in SMART stands for 'Measurable.' A measurable goal is a goal that has a tangible way to track and monitor progress. Using Jane's example, having a minimum number of steps she wants to get in every day is a much more accurate metric of success than simply saying "I want to walk every day" or even saying "I want to walk 30 minutes a day." 5,000 steps speaks to both the quantity of time spent moving and the speed at which one would have to walk to get those 5,000 steps in in a thirty minute period.

Victory occurs only when we can track our way to goal success.

In other words, you don't know if the strategies you're using work if you can't, as you use those strategies, measure their effectiveness. It saves a lot of wasted time and improper focus when you can set a goal that has clearly defined metrics that are trackable on a daily or weekly basis.

When you're thinking about making your goal measurable, you'll want to ask yourself:

- What are the milestones or smaller goal achievements that will need to happen to achieve the bigger goal?
- At what point, in my goal journey, should these milestones be happening?
- What are the daily and weekly activities that need to occur in order to achieve those smaller milestones?

Now... depending on the goal, you won't necessarily know all of the milestones associated with a goal. Give it your best guess and then create progress trackers that hold you accountable for entering in updates. The key is to schedule time at least once a week to update your progress trackers, review what's working and not working, and experiment with new strategies as is necessary. If a goal is not measurable, problems with your strategies of implementation will not be found quickly and you could end up spending far too long using an ineffective strategy because you didn't monitor whether or not it was working.

Let's walk through an example. If Matt has a goal of increasing his salary this year, my first question for Matt would be this: By how much do you want to increase your salary? Matt might then say "I'd like a 20% raise by the end of this year." If Matt's currently making $100,000/year, he is setting a goal of increasing his salary to $120,000/year by the end of this year. My next question for Matt would be "How do you plan to increase your salary by 20%?" Matt might then say "There's this IT certification that I want to get and, once I have it, I can apply for a different position at my company and those starting salaries are AT LEAST 20% higher than my current salary."

Okay, now we're in business!

At this point, the measuring of the goal of increasing his salary moves from the actual salary to the first step to increasing that salary- the earning of the

IT credential. If we were going to measure that, we'd now want to break down the curriculum for the IT credential (assuming he can easily pay for and sign up for it now) and create a study plan where he identifies how much of the credential program he'll get done each week, how many months it'll take to complete the certification training, pass the exam, and earn the credential. With his salary increase goal, our 'measurability' is all about getting that IT credential which would then lead to applying for positions in the other department which would naturally lead to that salary increase. Now… before we even go into measuring the IT credential completion process, we'd want to step back and ask a few questions:

> Does Matt have enough time, this year, to both complete the IT certification and apply for/get a new position?

> Once he's slated to complete the certification, what happens if no job openings in that department are available? Is Matt willing to look outside his organization for jobs paying at least $120,000/year or would it be possible for Matt to receive a promotion in his current role to $120,000/year?

> If Matt gets the certification but doesn't get the job that increases his salary to $120,000/year by the end of the year, what would be the next goal deadline? Or would the goal need to shift (something we'll talk about in Chapter 9)?

Once again, being able to measure your progress on a goal is important. What is also critically important is knowing which milestone of a goal to measure when. In Matt's case, the most important milestone to measure right now is the completion of the IT certification, not how many job openings currently exist in that other department that he'd like to go to.

Achievable

When I first learned the SMART framework in my MBA program at Auburn University, the A stood for 'Attainable.' Current literature identifies the A as standing for 'Achievable.' In other words, the goal you set needs to be a goal that's within the realm of attainability for you. Do you have the skills needed to achieve the goal by the date you've set? Are there skills or talents you'd need to build first in order to achieve the goal? The goal we walked through with Matt is a great example of a goal (earning

$120,000/year by the end of the year) where skills have to be acquired (i.e. getting the IT certification) before that goal can be met.

Achievable is about creating a goal that's challenging, yes, but not impossible for you to attain. If you have a goal to lose 100 pounds and you set the deadline for three months from now, given the timeframe, that goal is not achievable. If you set the weight loss goal for two years from now, the goal becomes what we call 'achievable.' The key to this piece of the SMART framework comes in accurately estimating how much time, effort, and experience you'll need to bring to a goal in order to achieve it by the timeframe you've set. Being sure that you are both equipped to do that work and complete that work by the deadline are what decide whether the goal is (or isn't) achievable.

You might be reading this and wondering "What's wrong with setting seemingly impossible goals? Doesn't the cliché say 'Shoot for the stars and at least you'll land on the moon?' And I hear that. However, one of the biggest crushers of self-belief and self-esteem comes in not following through on the commitments you make to yourself. If you develop the habit of NOT achieving your goals, after a while, you start to believe that you ARE a person who lacks the capacity to achieve the goals you've set. Now, a problem with goal setting gets confused with being your identity. You don't want to have to unravel that... which is why creating achievable goals- goals that stretch you but don't unravel you- becomes so important.

Relevant

When I first learned the SMART framework as an MBA student, the 'R' stood for 'Realistic.' It now stands for 'Relevant' which, in this case, means that the goal has to be a goal that carries some weight in the grander scheme of your life. Going after arbitrary goals that don't have a very strong WHY to them is a very fast way to not do the work of achieving that goal. Instead, you want to be sure that the goal you create is one that feeds into a larger goal or theme in your life. This is where knowing your life priorities becomes really important.

Going back to Chapter 2, this is the reason I asked you to list your top ten life goals. Once you have a clear idea of what those top ten life goals are, you're able to create goals with the expectation that each of those goals feed into one of those top ten goals… But, you have to know what your top life priorities are in order to do that.

Let's use an example to distinguish the difference between a relevant and an irrelevant goal. Elizabeth has a major life goal of buying her first home by her 35th birthday which will be in three years. Elizabeth also has a goal of buying her dream car, a Ferrari, in the next 10 years. Now… Elizabeth could work on saving the money for her Ferrari starting now. But, she would have to ask herself "What matters more at 33- saving up for the down payment on my house (20%) or buying that Ferrari? Which takes priority?"

Given that Elizabeth could buy herself a Ferrari at 60 and given the fact that she's set a goal to buy her first home in three years, clearly, the savings goal Elizabeth needs to set is about saving the 20% down payment for the house, not the $300,000 cost of a Ferrari… and if a 'starter' home where Elizabeth lives is in the ballpark of $500,000, she needs to save $100,000 to have that 20% deposit in three years… which boils down to saving approximately $34,000 a year for the next three years ($2,834/month). Again, it's about relevance… and only Elizabeth can decide if, for her life, saving almost $3,000/month is more relevant for the buying a house goal… or for the buying a $300,000 Ferrari goal.

The most important thing to remember about setting a relevant goal is this- you need to constantly ask yourself "How much does THIS goal matter to my life priorities?" It's a question you want to ask consistently through the goal setting process. It's so easy to get caught up in what other people want for you and, at times, it'll get confusing. You'll find yourself asking "So… is this a goal I REALLY want… or is this something other people think I 'should' want?" Don't be fooled into taking on goals other people think will be in your best interest. Constantly come back to the question and make sure that you can absolutely say that the goal you're going after is the goal that's most important to your life right now and in the long term.

Time Bound

There is nothing more demotivating than setting a deadline for a goal and not meeting (or exceeding) the deadline and, yet, for most people who feel like they suck at goal setting, this is typically the reason they feel this way. Goals can be extremely solid in terms of being specific, measurable, achievable and relevant but if the timeframe you set the goal up on is not realistic, it will dash the positive impact of all the other factors.

And here's where things get tricky- it takes experience, experimentation and practice to learn how to precisely and accurately set the timing of your goals. You won't necessarily get the goal deadline right the first fifty times you set a massive goal. The key to getting good at the 'Time Bound' aspect of goal setting is to do a great job of tracking the time you spend on each of the activities leading up to achieving each goal so, over time, you know exactly how much time it takes to achieve a similar goal. When you go to set that similar goal, you now have historical data that can tell you how long achieving that goal is going to take.

For example, the last time I focused on a fitness transformation and lost 60 pounds, what I learned, through a lot of trial and error and tracking, is this: My body tends to lose 2 lbs/week... no matter what. Now... could I force it to lose 3 pounds a week? Maybe... if I do extreme things. But, in all likelihood, if I'm following a normal program, my body is going to drop 2 lbs/week so, when I go to do another fitness transformation, I can use the historical data from the last time and focus on a 2 lb/week weight loss goal, knowing that the deadline I come up with will be realistic.

If you're setting a goal that's on a level you've never gone after before, a different strategy for getting Time Bound correct lives in overestimating (oftentimes, overestimating a lot) how long you think it's going to take to get to the goal. Whenever I'm pursuing a goal I've never pursued before, I typically double or triple the time I think it's going to take to achieve the goal and use that as my goal deadline... and you'd be surprised by how often I get to the goal achievement and realize I probably should've quadrupled the amount of time I allotted to achieving the goal. Don't be afraid to triple or quadruple the amount of time you think it's going to take you to get to a goal. What's the worst thing that could happen? You under promise and overdeliver to yourself. That's a win-win.

Now… there will be those who say "But if you give yourself too much time, doesn't that make you complacent? Doesn't the sense of urgency create the momentum and push you need to make the goal happen in a very tight time frame?" And here's my answer: sometimes. It depends how realistic (or unrealistic) the deadline is. If you know it takes you two years to write a book, setting a goal of writing a book in three months is not going to create so much urgency that you actually end up writing a book in three months. That simply isn't enough time… and… there are many other ways to create a sense of urgency around your goals without setting unrealistic timelines. However, if it takes you two years to write a book and you decide to set the deadline for eighteen months, that could put you in a position to feel a deep sense of urgency that then forces you to be more efficient and productive AND get the book done in eighteen months.

Bottom line- track all the time you spend working on each goal so you have historical data that can inform goal setting in the future so that, as time passes, you set goals with both accuracy and precision.

Goal Setting Approach #2: The 6 Ws of Goal Setting

You'll find the 6Ws approach embedded in all of the other goal setting approaches. It's the process of asking 6 W questions:
1. Who needs to be involved with achieving this goal?
2. What exactly are you trying to accomplish with this goal?
3. When will you work on and complete this goal?
4. Where will you work on this goal?
5. Which factors will impact your ability to achieve this goal?
6. Why does this goal matter?

Let's look at each question separately.

1: Who needs to be involved with achieving this goal?

Is this goal completely up to you? Are there coaches, mentors, or partners who will help you achieve this goal? What resources and support will you need in order to accomplish this goal?

2: *What exactly are you trying to accomplish with this goal?*

What are the results that will be obtained by achieving this goal? What does 'done' look like in terms of this goal? What's the metric of success for this goal? In this way, you want to lay out all of the results you expect to experience as a result of achieving the goal.

3: *When will you work on and complete this goal?*

It's one thing to create a goal. It's quite another to make sure that you have the time, energy and bandwidth required to attain the goal within the allotted timeframe. Having a clear idea of what days/times, weeks, and months you'll work on a particular goal will give you a sense of whether the goal can feasibly be achieved within the timeframe you set.

4: *Where will you work on this goal?*

Very often, the achievement of big goals requires laser focus… and laser focus is best cultivated in an environment of quiet, calm, and few distractions. Answering the question "Where will I work on this goal?" is a great way to assess if you have the environment (or need to create the environment) required to get the most out of productivity so you can reach the goal.

5: *Which factors will impact your ability to achieve this goal?*

Understanding the landscape of your goal is a critical piece of putting yourself in the best position to achieve the goal. The landscape includes any factors that can negatively or positively impact your ability to achieve the goal. For example, let's say your goal is to start eating clean. For the last five years, you've eaten a pretty unhealthy diet. Before you pick a certain nutrition plan or go meal prep shopping, there are a number of factors you may want to take into consideration, including:

- Your partner and kids eat a lot of junk food and have no intentions of jumping on the 'clean eating' bandwagon
- You work 10 hour shifts six days a week and you barely take breaks so you wind up eating one or two meals most days
- Because you sleep less than 6 hours a night, you feel exhausted most of the time and lean on caffeine and sugar as ways to get through each day

- You're on a very tight budget and eating higher protein and more veggies is definitely out of your grocery budget range

Now… even though you know this is the goal you want to go after, the factors we just went through must be taken into consideration before you A- confirm that this is going to be your goal and B- create a plan that works around all of the previously mentioned constraints. A lot of people will avoid looking at the factors that impact going after a goal. They fear that those 'factors' will discourage them from going after the goal. On the contrary, knowing the landscape of the goal territory you're working on enables you to develop a more solid plan for achieving the goal.

6: *Why does this goal matter?*

When it comes to achieving a big goal that exists on a level you've never achieved before, the WHY is the momentum driver to the WHAT. In other words, knowing WHY you're pursuing a goal (how much it matters, why it matters, and the impact achieving this goal will have on your life and the life of others) is critical to staying the course on the goal, especially when you face obstacles that cause you to question whether you have what it takes to achieve the goal.

Goal Setting Approach #3: PACT Method

While SMART goals focus on the expected outcome desired, PACT is a goal setting method that focuses on the factors required to successfully achieve any goal. PACT stands for:

- Purposeful
- Actionable
- Continuous
- Trackable

This method of goal setting is about the pursuit of goal depth rather than a total focus on creating goals associated with big achievements.

Let's take a deeper look at each of the components to PACT:

- **Purposeful:** For a goal to be achieved, it has to mean something to you. It's got to be something that has a long term, positive impact on your life. It also has to be something that will serve you in the long term, something that aligns with the future you desire. While a short-term goal might feel interesting, if it doesn't have long term impact, it won't be compelling... and you won't stay the course when the going gets tough. The question to determine if a goal you've set is purposeful is this- How will achieving this goal change my life in 10 years? If the answer is "It won't", the goal isn't purposeful (or not purposeful enough).

- **Actionable:** A solid goal is one that can be traced from beginning to end with action. In other words, can you write out a recipe that includes all of the actions it will take to get to your goal... or is the goal so vague and fluid that you aren't able to clearly come up with deliverables or milestones that need to happen in order to achieve the goal? For example, if your goal is "to be happy", what specific actions lead to that? I'm sure you can come up with a few but couldn't you come up with more well-defined deliverables if, instead of saying "My goal is to be happy", your goal was to engage in at least one joy-producing activity each month? The latter goal is specific enough that you could easily create a map or recipe for how to achieve the goal.

- **Continuous:** If you've ever found yourself in a place where you wiffle waffle between goals, you understand what a goal that is NOT continuous looks like. When there are too many options for goal setting and a lot of confusion about 'which goal' is the 'right' goal, people tend to fall prey to things like analysis paralysis (i.e. making no decision because of the overwhelm of information) or decision fatigue (feeling too tired to make any more decisions because so many tiny decisions have already been made). In the PACT method, a good goal is continuous. It's not simply a flavor-of-the-month, shiny object goal that feels really exciting because it's new but loses all focus once another new, shiny goal comes into view. It's a goal that you're willing to work on, even if progress is slow and even if there are many tweaks you have to make to your goal achievement strategy along the way. It's continuous because you focus on improving and getting closer to the goal rather than taking an "I've got to get to the goal right now or else go to something else!" mentality.

- **Trackable:** By far, the most interesting and compelling variable in the PACT method of goal setting is the emphasis placed on a goal being trackable. It's not enough to say "I got the result" but how often are you consistently taking Daily Massive Action (DMA)? How is your consistent, daily progress coming along and what methods are you using to track your follow through on a daily basis? A great goal comes along with an effective, simple method of tracking consistent progress.

Goal Setting Approach #4: The ONE Thing

While The ONE Thing is not a goal setting approach per se, what it represents is a powerful way by which to set the goals that matter most to you. In his book <u>The ONE Thing</u>, Gary Keller points out the following:

"To achieve an extraordinary result, you must choose what matters most and give it all the time it demands. This requires getting extremely out of balance in relation to all other work issues, with only infrequent counterbalancing to address them."

He goes on to say "In your professional life, go long and make peace with the idea that the pursuit of extraordinary results may require you to be out of balance for long periods."

Keller presents what he calls the **focusing question** which is the core philosophy of the book. He recommends asking yourself this question consistently to make sure that you're creating and staying focused on the goals that matter most.

Here's the focusing question:
What's the ONE Thing I can do such that by doing it, everything else will be easier or unnecessary?

You might be wondering "How does The ONE Thing relate to goal setting?" And here's the answer- One of the biggest problems people have with setting goals comes in figuring out which goals take priority. Two questions come to mind in this dilemma:

- What goal matters most?

- In what order should I be pursuing my goals?

When you add the focusing question to your approach to goal setting, all of a sudden, you get VERY clear on your #1 goal AND you get crystal clear on which goal has to come first... all at the same time.

Here's the other powerful point about using The ONE Thing in your goal setting: By answering the focusing question, you now know where the bulk of your focus blocks and attention needs to go UNTIL you get this ONE Thing achieved. It really helps with laser focus and goal commitment because, now, you're not trying to multi-task (multi-tasking is not something humans do). Now, you're getting clear on the fact that you have to decide your ONE Thing and give all of your time to that... UNTIL it's achieved. That changes the game for how you approach taking DMA (Daily Massive Action).

One note: Before you integrate the focusing question into your goal setting approach, I highly recommend you read Gary Keller's book. There are a lot of nuances that he goes over in the book so read it for the full context of how to apply the question to your goals.

Goal Setting Approach #5: Brian Tracy's Seven Step Process for Achieving Goals
In his book Just Shut Up and Do it! 7 Steps to Conquer Your Goals, Brian Tracy lays out a seven-step process for achieving goals.

Here's an overview of the goal setting method:
- **Step #1:** Decide exactly what you want in each area of your life.
- **Step #2:** Write the goal down, clearly and in detail.
- **Step #3:** Set a specific deadline (break it down into sub-deadlines and write them in the order of operations for a large goal).
- **Step #4:** Make a list of all of the actions that will have to be taken to achieve the goal.
- **Step #5:** Organize the items on your list into a plan by placing them in the proper sequence and priority.
- **Step #6:** Take immediate action on the most important thing you can do on your plan.

- **Step #7:** Do something every day that moves you towards the attainment of one or more of your goals (i.e. keep the momentum going).

In the <u>Own Your Goals Planner Pack</u>, I've included a goal clarity training session that helps you get clear about what you want so completing the above seven steps can be done with ease. In the meantime, let's take a closer look at each step.

Step #1: Decide exactly what you want.
Do you have a clear idea of what you want in each area of your life, so clear that you could explain your goals to a five-year-old and that five-year-old could both understand and repeat back to you the goals, what you'd have to do to achieve them, and how they'd know that you got the results? Can you do that? If you can't, the goal isn't specific enough.

Step #2: Write the goal down.
Write your goal down in a journal. Re-read your goals (or re-write your goals) on a daily basis. This helps to reinforce what your daily priorities are and it also helps you notice when you start to get distracted by daily activities that are not leading you to those goals.

Step #3: Set specific deadlines.
We will talk more about this in the chapter on goal management but here's the gist- you have to put your goals and dreams on a timeline so you know what needs to happen by when. While both the plan and the due dates will change, the importance of having those specific deadlines has little to do with holding yourself to rigid timelines and everything to do with being able to assess, on a daily basis, how good your follow through is, how well you're able to flex and flow with life, and what you need to do to become more precise and intentional in your contingency planning. Specific deadlines give you something to work towards while also giving you data on how to set future deadlines with more precision.

Step #4: Make a list of all of the actions that will have to be taken to achieve the goal.

One of the biggest mistakes people make when it comes to achieving goals comes when they dismiss the exploration and brainstorming process and, instead, dive right into goal setting. Do not rob yourself of the creativity, imagination, and fun that can be had by asking (and giving yourself plenty of time and space to answer) the question: "What *could* I do to achieve this goal?" Give yourself the permission and freedom to write down every possible thing you could do to achieve this goal.

Step #5: Organize the items on your list into a plan by placing them in the proper sequence and priority.

Once you've completed Step #4, you're ready to organize all of those wonderful ideas into a list of action items that are arranged by sequence and priority. Look at the brainstorming list you've got and ask yourself "Which of these action steps would need to come first, second and third? What's the priority for today, this week, this month?" In this way, when you identify what matters most and take care of that first, it creates a domino effect in terms of both momentum and priority so you end up getting more done in less time.

Step #6: Take immediate action on the most important thing you can do on your plan. A plan is great but it means nothing if you don't take action on it. It's so easy to spend days, weeks and even months developing this gorgeous plan… only to tuck it away somewhere and find it while cleaning a year or two later and wonder "Why didn't I ever do something with that?" The best way to avoid planning without action comes in MAKING yourself take immediate action on the plan AS SOON AS the plan has been developed. Literally take one next step the moment you've finished the plan.

Step #7: Do something every day that moves you towards the attainment of one or more of your goals (i.e. keep the momentum going). It's not enough to take one immediate action. If you're going to get to your goal, you'll need to take at least one Daily Massive Action (DMA) in the direction of your goal or dream. It is the frequency and the consistency of action that sustains momentum over a long period of time. Make it a non-negotiable that you take action on your goals every single day.

Tracy's goal setting approach is a comprehensive, straight forward way to set goals. It provides a step-by-step process to clearly identify what you want to achieve in a way that organizes things by sequence and priority. The downside to this goal setting method is that it doesn't work very well for individuals who feel unclear about what they want in each area of their lives. It's also a challenging approach to use for an individual who knows what they want but feels torn about the competing priorities of goals in different life arenas.

At the end of the day, most goal setting approaches work IF you work them. The key to working any goal setting approach consistently is its alignment with how you move through life. It's imperative that you find or create a goal setting approach that works for YOU... and if you come to a place where you say to yourself "No goal setting approach works for me", keep in mind that one of two things will have to happen in that circumstance:

1. You change yourself so that you are committed to and able to align with a goal setting strategy at some point.
2. You create a unique goal setting strategy that proves to you (in 3 months' time) that it is best suited to how you move through life.

Either way, you've got to find a goal setting strategy and it's got to be a strategy that works. That will require that either you change or the strategy changes... Notice I didn't mention the goal changing. When you know what you want, the intended result DOES NOT change. How you get there will. How long it takes definitely will. But, your desire to achieve the goal will not waiver when the goal you set is actually the goal you TRULY want AND believe you can have.

CHAPTER 8: HAVE YOU MET YOUR FUTURE SELF?

Allow yourself to grow and change. Your Future Self is waiting."
- Unknown

On almost a daily basis, I spend some amount of time talking to my Future Self. Sometimes, I sit in my meditation chair, close my eyes, and visualize myself asking her for guidance and mentoring. In those situations, I usually see her in a big white kitchen. She's wearing a white workout outfit. She's super fit, in her early 50s, and she's so happy… and when I ask her questions, she's extremely matter-of-fact, blunt even and her words, most of the time, cut to the bone because it's what I know the answer is but what I fight to accept and follow through on. So she tells the truth and I receive it… and then I get out of the visualization and say to myself "Damn… I guess I better listen."

Other times, I'll be driving somewhere or planning my day and I'll stop and ask myself "How would my Future Self handle this situation or live out this day? How would my Future Self solve this problem?" I then outline the answers I get and do my best to line up with handling things the way my Future Self would.

I also try to move through my day asking "How does my Future Self feel in her life and what can I do to feel that way today?" My Future Self feels fulfilled, powerful, vibrant, vivacious, focused, beautiful, on fire in life and ready to seize the day. She feels abundant and in charge. She feels confident and relaxed. She feels like the boss and she says what she means and means what she says. She is kind but clear. She feels loving and loved. She doesn't give a rat's ass what anybody else thinks and feels so free because of that fact. On an average day, she's writing, working out, and taking her horse into the mountains. She loves nature and she takes it in on a daily basis. She's wise and energetically powerful. She radiates joy, love, and achievement. She doesn't back down and she doesn't give up. She moves, flows, and gets what she wants."

When I think about everything I just described, it leaves my Current Self in my Future Self's shoes. I now feel that way in this moment. I now bask in the power and the vibrancy and vivaciousness of that 50/60 year old me and I radiate that kind of energy now... and I'm able to tap into that because I've met my Future Self. I spend time consistently with my Future Self. I talk to my Future Self. I listen to my Future Self. And, even in moments when I feel so far from who she is, I remind myself that that version of me is inside of me right now just waiting for me to embody her.

But, you can't embody a version of you you've never met or are unwilling to get to know. You certainly can't embody a version of you that you don't believe is possible for you. So the question becomes "Have you met your Future Self?" If the answer is No, it's time to do that...

How do you Meet Your Future Self?

You meet your Future Self the same way you'd meet a potential romantic partner on an online dating site- you read their profile. In your Future Self's case, you need to create your Future Self's profile. Whether you journal it or you do a visualization for 15 minutes, sit with yourself and design how you want the version of you that will exist in 10 years to look, feel and operate.

To get really clear on your Future Self profile, ask and answer the following questions.

In 10 years' time:
- ➢ Who do I want to be?
- ➢ How do I look?
- ➢ Where do I live?
- ➢ What does an average day look and feel like for me?
- ➢ How do I wake up?
- ➢ How do I go to bed?
- ➢ What's my mindset like?
- ➢ What are the thoughts I think about consistently?
- ➢ What line of work am I in?
- ➢ How does my body look?
- ➢ How do I eat?

- What is my friend group like?
- Who's in my tribe?
- Who am I romantically connected to?
- What does my family look like?
- What do I do for fun?
- What are my weekends like?
- How often do I travel?
- What is my house like and how is it decorated?
- What do my healthy boundaries look like?
- How do I speak to myself?
- How do I talk to other people?
- What kinds of people do I attract?
- What kinds of people do I not allow into my inner circle?
- What forms of media do I spend time looking at or consuming?
- How much time do I spend in nature?
- What does my money look like?
- What level of wealth am I at?
- How does my savings account look?
- What's my FICO score?
- What dreams do I have that I want to accomplish at that point in my life?
- What have I accomplished over the next ten years?
- What am I most proud of?
- What relationships do I invest the most in?
- What is my spirituality like and how do I practice it?
- What is my relationship to my community?
- Where do I feel I most belong?
- What's my workout routine like?
- How often do I practice self-care and in what ways?
- How do I handle negative emotion?
- How do I deal with obstacles?
- How do I solve problems?
- What's my energy like?
- What am I proud of myself for?
- How have I made peace with being who I am?

And these questions are a starter list. They will help you get really clear on who your Future Self is… and use your imagination. Don't limit yourself to some projection of who you think it's possible to become given who you currently are. Dr. Benjamin Hardy puts it beautifully when he says "Your future self is not someone you discover, but someone you decide to be."

Get clear on who your Future Self is… and don't think that she has to be a perfect person. Your Future Self is brilliant and it's not because she's perfect; it's because she consistently shows up as her most powerful Self. Consistency, yes. Perfection, no.

Here's the other piece to understand about envisioning your Future Self. **You will never be the same person twice in a lifetime.** Read that again and take it in. In other words, your entire life is an evolution. The goal was never and will never be to arrive at a 'finished' version of yourself. The goal is not to hit a Future Self destination; it's to evolve and unfold into every new version of you and a new version of you will exist in every moment of every day for the rest of your life.

Another thing to consider- you are NOT your personality. These labels that we give ourselves (i.e. "I'm an introvert, extrovert, shy, loud, the black sheep of the family, a handy person, not handy, outdoorsy, hate computers") are so limiting. And they are not meant to last forever. Just because you were a shy kid doesn't mean your fate is to grow up and become a hermit as an adult. While there are personality tendencies and some research that correlates to that nature (rather than nurture) determines your disposition, none of that means that your personality can't or won't change. You have power over that too so don't limit yourself by giving your 'personality' more power than it should have.

Instead, imagine the Future Self you want to be. Define the personality, attitude, behaviors, and characteristics of that version of you. Then begin embodying that Future Self today. Wake up every day and ask yourself "What's one action I could take today that would fully embody my Future Self?" Maybe it's a workout. Maybe it's meditation. Maybe it's reading a book. It doesn't have to be big; it simply needs to be something you do to align with your Future Self on a daily basis.

To successfully achieve your goals in the shortest amount of time possible, you need to be deeply connected to your future Self. The story you tell yourself about you has to line up with the vision you journaled of your Future Self which then has to also line up with the thoughts you think and the actions you take on a daily basis… and that also means being vigilant about putting your former selves where they belong- in the past.

One of the fastest ways to crush your connection to your Future Self comes in holding your Current Self hostage by replaying all of the mistakes your past selves have made. There's nothing you can do to change past mistakes. You have no ability to go back in time and do it all differently. However, you do have the ability to tell a new story about the past you lived, to learn the lessons and apply them as your Current Self and to hold yourself to the higher standards of your Future Self. Yes, you can do all of those things which does require pushing through levels of discomfort. You have to break out of comfort zones in order to live as your Future Self. You have to tell yourself the new story of who you are over and over again, even when you don't believe it and especially when you don't see how you're going to get to that version of you. You have to define your moment-by-moment decisions by the person you're becoming and not by the safety of the person you've always been… and all of this takes time, dedication, and the willingness to stay the course… all of which you can do IF you believe you can.

Practice being your Future Self at least one time a day. Take one action or one step that your Future Self would and then add more actions as the weeks pass by. Build the connection to your Future Self by spending 5-7 minutes in quiet contemplation and visualization of a day in the life of that Future You. Savor in the seeing and being of it. Let every aspect of what you see inform what you get up and do next. The stronger your connection today to your Future Self, the faster you'll get to that version of you.

Most importantly, remember to take actions on your goals, not as your current self but with all of the power, focus and confidence of your Future Self. Step into that version of you BEFORE you take the action and notice how different the goal taking action feels and how different the level of progress and performance is as a result.

Your Future Self IS here right now and that Future Self IS you. Operate and act from that perspective...

CHAPTER 9: THE ART AND SCIENCE OF REVERSE ENGINEERING YOUR GOALS

You can't expect to succeed if you only
put in work on the days that you feel like it.
- Unknown

In Chapter 8, we talked about meeting and aligning with your Future Self. That was great preparation for what we're going to discuss in Chapter 9… which is the art and science of reverse engineering your goals. If you look on the web, there are many definitions of reverse engineering. Let me give you the definition we're going to work with in this book:

Reverse Engineering is a method by which we work backwards from a desired end result to take apart all of the milestones, steps, and activities that led to the achievement of the end result. In this way, we deconstruct an outcome to get more insight into all of the actions that led to the achievement of that outcome.

In layman's terms, we're going to work backwards. We're going to start with you having already achieved the goal, ask the question "How did I get to the goal?" and walk through all of the steps our Future Selves took to get to that accomplishment, thereby laying out a blueprint for achieving that goal.

What's the Purpose of Reverse Engineering a Goal?

Reverse engineering goals is a powerful way to 1- set goals as your Future Self, 2- Get clear on all the steps you believe it's going to take to get to the goal and 3- Set doable timelines for achieving the goal based on what you learn through the reverse engineering process.

Chapter 8 laid out the process for stepping into and embodying your Future Self. Now that you know how to do that, we can move forward and, from the perspective of your Future Self, walk through the process of learning how to reverse engineer your goals.

How do you Reverse Engineer a Goal?

Reverse engineering a goal involves a four-step process:

✓ *Step #1: Clearly define your actual goal.* What is the end state or outcome that you're going for? Be sure that it's a clear result that can be measured (so you know when you actually hit the goal).

✓ *Step #2: Ask the reverse engineering question.* Sitting in the mindset of your Future Self, imagine that you've achieved the goal and ask and answer the question "What milestones did I have to reach in order to achieve this goal?" Write down all the steps that came.

✓ *Step #3: Identify the action steps under each milestone.* Under each of the steps you listed, identify key action steps or deliverables that would have to be taken to get to each of the milestones you identified.

✓ *Step #4: Create a starting point plan.* Now that you've reverse engineered the key milestones and action steps that led to the goal, it's time to identify your current starting point and identify what your next three steps are. What are the next three pivotal steps that you can take to reach that very first milestone to your goal? Write down the next three steps and get up and take immediate action.

What I just walked you through is the 'science' of reverse engineering. You now have the steps to do it but the successful doing of it has a lot of 'art' to it... Meaning- it's not enough to walk through the steps. You've got to be able to get into the mindset and perspective of your Future Self BEFORE you engage in the reverse engineering process and certainly while you're taking the actions that have come out of that process... and that can be hard for a lot of people to consistently do.

You have to consciously think differently about this goal. You can't think about it in the way you would as your Current Self. You almost have to rise above the Current Self and say "Okay, my Future Self has already achieved this. My Future Self KNOWS that this goal is as good as done. My Future Self has found a great way to go about getting this done. Let me tap into that insight and wisdom and look at the goal journey differently..."

This requires stepping into your Future Self's shoes. I like to tell coaching clients that it's like being an actor who dives into a new role. To adequately prepare to take on the role, the actor will do all sorts of things to embody the character. He'll create a character biography. She'll dress and walk through life for several weeks as that character. He'll speak with that dialect, eat the foods his character would eat and go to places his character would go to. It is the immersion of an actor into the lived experience of that character that then enables the actor to play the part beautifully. You can apply a similar approach to embodying your Future Self as you do the reverse engineering.

For the next 24 hours, put on the 'character' of your Future Self. Walk, talk, dress, behave and act like the Future version of you that you're going for. Be reasonable about this. Do what's possible in the now with your Future Self. But, think the thoughts, say the things, and move through your day for 24 hours as that future version of you. Then… sit down for three to four hours and reverse engineer one or more of your goals. Having lived as your Future Self for 24 hours, you are close enough to that version of you that, when you reverse engineer your goals, you'll naturally slip into that Future Self perspective.

What if you try to reverse engineer your goal and you come up with nothing?

I've gotten that question a lot. A person will say to me "But, I've never achieved anything on the level of achieving this goal. I have no idea how to reverse engineer it and, when I follow the process, I come up with nothing." And here are three things you can do when you attempt the reverse engineering process and you're not producing anything:

1. **Google 'How to achieve…' whatever your goal is.** Someone has achieved what you're trying to achieve. Google and read blog posts, stories, and watch YouTube videos from people who've accomplished what you want to accomplish. Remember: There is nothing new under the sun. Find others who've done it, learn their steps and apply their steps to your reverse engineering process.

2. **Learn from your past goal achievement processes.** Think about a goal you achieved that is on the closest level to this goal. What was your process for achieving that? Apply the same approach (albeit different techniques) to this goal.

3. **Make an educated guess.** At some point, rather than remaining stuck in the "I don't know how to do this" frame of mind, it's better to be decisive and simply guess how achieving this goal could go. At least you now have a framework from which to operate and you'll change strategy and process along the way... which happens with every goal you pursue, whether you've achieved something similar to it or not.

At the end of the day, reverse engineering your goals is an experiment in developing a path and a plan to that goal. Do not overthink this. It is far more important for you to show up to the reverse engineering process being decisive and clear about your ability to reverse engineer than it is coming to the process feeling like you have this reverse engineering down to a science.

Let me help you out: NO ONE has reverse engineering down to a science. This is about experimenting, learning, failing, iterating, trying something different and then doing the process all over again. You will get from the reverse engineering process what you put into it. Go into the process saying to yourself "I know what I want. I know I can get there. I'm going to experiment and try different things. I'm going to learn the best way for me to achieve this goal and that's the point of doing this." It's about being decisive in who you are and how you are choosing to show up to the process.

Any process will work when you show up to it believing in your ability to get the most out of the process. Believe in yourself. Show up decisively. Be willing to fail forward and grow. Reverse engineering works beautifully when you show up ready and willing to learn...

CHAPTER 10: GOAL SETTING 101

Nothing will work unless you do.
- Maya Angelou

How safe do you feel in your life?

It's not a common question to ask but it's one we should be asking on a consistent basis because your level of perceived safety will have a lot to do with your ability to go all in on achieving your goals… and I haven't heard many 'goal teachers' speak to the fact that psychological and physical safety **are** critical prerequisites to achieving goals.

And notice I didn't say it was a prerequisite to 'setting' goals. It's absolutely possible to feel totally unsafe and go into a massive goal setting mode because the goal setting, on some level, gives you a false sense of security. Lots of people do that.

But, here's what I want to get very clear on before we dive into the goal setting process I'm going to share with you in this chapter- You will not achieve a goal in any environment you don't feel safe enough in to devote the time, put forth the effort, and trust the process for long enough to do the ALL IN work of getting to the goal.

Let me put this another way:
Unless and until you feel safe enough in your life to pursue the goals in your heart, you will sabotage your efforts, shortcut your process, and get distracted by the life fires you feel you need to put out because, deep down, you don't feel safe enough to give yourself permission to focus completely on the achievement of the goal.

And it's a tricky thing because we see success stories of people who grew up under horrendous conditions and achieved an unreal level of success and we say "Okay, so if that person could pull themselves out of such horrible conditions and get to their goals, what's my problem?"

Here's the thing you're missing about that success story: For that person, the safest thing they could do, in that horrible situation, was put ALL of their focus on achieving the goals because that person knew that achieving that goal was the ONLY way they were going to survive. So, for that person, the safety was in pursuing and achieving the goal.

And a lot of us don't have that "Achieve this goal or horrible things will happen to me" feeling nor do we want or need to have that in our mindsets to achieve a goal. I'm not proposing that you scare the hell out of yourself in order to go ALL IN on your goals. What I am saying is that you need to take a step back, before you set goals, and really assess where you are in your life and how safe you feel in going after the goals you set.

If you don't feel safe enough to do the work and stay the course on your goals, at some point, you're going to give up. The only way you will stay the course is if you feel like you have just enough safety to pour yourself into this goal without having the rest of your life fall apart as a result. That sounds super dramatic but, if you really sit with the thoughts you're having about going after a big goal, a lot of the fear comes from this "running from a saber tooth tiger" fight-or-flight mentality so many of us live in.

So I'm going to start this chapter helping you figure out where you stand with safety and whether or not the goals you want to set align with the level of safety that you're at. Then we'll get into what I call the **TRUST goal setting process**. Let's begin by level setting on what you're going to walk away with after reading this chapter.

In this chapter, you're going to learn how to:
1. Get clear on where you are with your current level of safety.
2. Identify what season of life you're in and decide what matters most to you in THIS season of life.
3. Understand the four quadrants of life (health, wealth, relationships, spirituality) and where your goal setting biases lie.
4. Avoid and/or get out of the most common goal setting traps.
5. Review my TRUST process for goal setting.

Where is Your Level of Safety?

Abraham Maslow (1908-1970) was an American theorist who operated from the perspective of humanistic psychology. As one of the founders of humanistic psychology (1950s), Maslow believed that people are innately good and that problems arise when people stray from that innate goodness. Humanistic psychology believes strongly in each person's ability to choose their lives and goes on to say that every person is motivated to use their agency to achieve their full potential, to self-actualize. Humanistic psychology believes that the need for fulfillment and personal growth are serious sources of motivation for human beings and that the search for personal growth and evolution is a lifelong process because all people want to become better, stronger, wiser version of themselves.

Maslow is most well-known for the creation of Maslow's Hierarchy of Needs. First introduced in 1943 in a paper he wrote called "A Theory of Human Motivation", Maslow argued that people are motivated to fulfill their needs in a particular order and that, until basic needs are met, the focus on and quest for the fulfillment of higher-level needs will not be a priority for that individual.

The hierarchy of needs is shown below.

MASLOW'S HIERARCHY OF NEEDS

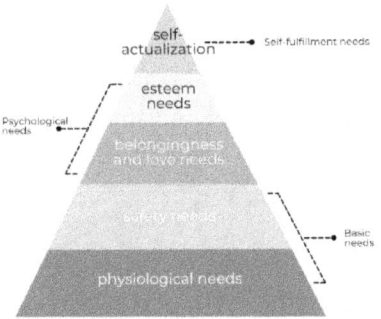

Physiological Needs: According to Maslow, physiological needs refer to making sure that a person has their basic needs met (air, water, food, shelter, sleep, clothing, sex and/or reproduction).

Safety Needs: Maslow defined safety needs as having personal security, employment, resources, health (physical and mental- including psychological safety), and property (not simply living somewhere but having a physical dwelling that is yours).

Love and Belonging Needs: According to Maslow, this level of need is about having solid friendships, romantic partnerships, family, intimacy, trust, acceptance and a deep sense of connection.

Esteem Needs: Maslow broke down esteem needs into two categories- 1) esteem for oneself (dignity, achievement, mastery, independence) and 2) the need to be accepted and valued by others (being respected, having status, recognition, and prestige from others).

Self-Actualization: As the highest point in the hierarchy of needs, Maslow felt that self-actualization occurs when a person fulfills their potential, has peak experiences and becomes the most they can be.

Maslow did update his model and, in the 1960s, brought in an even higher-level order need he called **Self-Transcendence** (above self-actualization). Self-transcendence occurs once a person has self-actualized. Now that the person is all he or she can be, the focus moves away from the self. Goals now focus on transcending the identity and pursuing goals that reach beyond that person and positively impact the world.

While there are many contemporary psychologists who argue (and rightly so) that this hierarchy of needs from the 1940s (and updates in the 1960s) still require some updating, here's where I want to connect the idea of safety to goal setting:

Before you can successfully set AND achieve goals, you need to assess where, on Maslow's hierarchy, you're currently living so you know which goals REQUIRE your time and focus in THIS season of your life.

And it makes sense. If you lost your job five months ago and haven't been able to find work, you're homeless and you're living in a car that's about to be repossessed, how could you possibly focus on a love and belonging goal like dating and meeting your soul mate, getting married, and having children when you're completely focused on surviving today and making it to tomorrow?

And physical safety isn't the only kind of safety that's needed. Especially in today's world, people NEED psychological safety, the feeling and belief that you can share your thoughts, opinions, and ideas freely without fear of being degraded or shamed.

It's important for you, prior to setting goals, to ask yourself "Where is my current level of physical and psychological safety?"

In other words:
- [ ] To what extent do I feel safe enough to pursue this goal?
- [ ] Does my home environment (physical layout, energy of the home, and people in the home) create an atmosphere where I feel like I have the space, time, and room to go ALL IN on my goals?
- [ ] Do I have enough emotional room to put and keep my focus on doing the work of achieving my goals?
- [ ] Am I surrounded by people who support my goals and dreams… or am I surrounded by emotional vampires that drain me?

How you answer those questions will determine what kinds of goals are the most important for where you are in this season of your life… and if you try to ignore what level of safety you're at and set goals that are far beyond what your current level of safety will allow, that's when you get into the vicious cycle of setting goals you don't achieve and feeling like a person who can't ever seem to get your goals on point.

What season of life are you in and what goals matter most to you in THIS season of life?

The safety question is intimately tied to the season of life you're in. I touched upon this a little bit in Chapter 5 but it's time to take a deeper dive into the seasons of life. While I pull this discussion from psychology's lifespan development theory (i.e. the concept that our lives break down to different stages such as early, middle, and late adulthood), I find many of these psychological theories deeply flawed, completely biased, and from a time and era that has long since past. So I want to talk about life seasons in a very different way, not based on age but based on season.

In nature, there are four seasons: spring, summer, fall, and winter. I'm not sure why most people have the tendency to say it as "Winter, spring, summer and fall" but the seasons traditionally start with spring. The magic of spring comes in the idea that this is a season where the world wakes up from a deep, dark slumber. The cold of winter makes way for the newness of life. Flowers bud. Daylight lasts longer. There's this feeling that the warmth and brightness of life has returned.

When we are in a spring season of life, it's a time of planting new seeds, experiencing new beginnings, of going on new adventures, of being open to and surrounded by the beauty of life. It's as if you're opening up and, as a result, life is responding by opening up to you. When you're in a spring season of life, you know it.

Summer is a fiery season of owning your power, using your potential, continuing to build the life you want while knowing that you're very close to reaping what you've sown. You continue to work and progress but you're doing so from a place of power. When you're in a summer season of life, you feel large and in charge. You have a clear vision and you feel like you're on the path doing the things you're supposed to do.

Autumn is the season where life is changing and, at the same time, you are reaping what you've sown. Change happens very fast in an autumn season. The things that felt sure and prominent in the summer are quickly fading into the changing of colors, the shorter days and the longer nights, the cooling of the temperatures. You can feel the need to allow change to happen and it becomes very clear that you can't control how fast or how much things change in this season. You are also starting to reflect on what you've reaped... and how what you've sown led to this place.

Winter is the final season of life and all the leaves have gone from the trees. This is the end of a cycle where things have died or gone away and you are left with yourself- in the cold, dark and with a deep desire to reflect, learn lessons, and to rest as you figure out what comes next. Winter is also the season where things are stripped down. They are bare and there could be very little for you to live off of. When you hear people like Tony Robbins say "Winter is coming", what he means is this- there is a time of hardship, cold, and dark coming. It is in the three seasons before that you are meant to work and prepare for the winter season that will involve having less and needing to go within to figure out what's next.

So you might be asking "Okay, how does the season of life I'm in affect my goal setting?" And here's the answer- you want to be sure that the goals you're setting A- take into consideration all four seasons and 2- Reflect the energy and strength of the current life season you're in.

Let me give you an example…

You might find yourself in a spring season of life. You've just moved to a new town or started a new job. New beginnings is the energy of your life right now. It makes sense, in this spring season, to think about the seeds you want to sow and the results you want to reap in the fall.

Maybe your new job is a brand-new career and you want to figure out how to move up in that career over the next two years. Your 'Autumn', in your mind, will happen in two years' time so you're creating a career goal lays out all the seeds you need to be planting and tending to in your career for the next two years to reap the level of promotion you want in the next twenty-four months.

But, what if you're someone who's in your mid-career and you just got laid off? You feel blindsided by being laid off. You know that, financially, this is going to be really rough. Guess what? You've just entered a winter season of life. There's much less available to you. You're in a state of hardship. You're in deep reflection about what went wrong, what now has to happen, and how you can get yourself out of this situation. You're in survival mode now… and that is what the winter season can feel like.

It can also feel like a simmering unhappiness with the current state of your life and feeling like you need to go within and figure out what's not working with your life and what needs to change so that, when spring comes again, you can plant the right seeds.

I'm not saying you can't plant seeds in the winter but the seeds will take and grow better when planted in the right season. I also think that you need to assess if the seeds you're planting in the spring season of your life will give you enough to provide for you whenever a winter season comes about (and it will show up). Are your spring seeds enough to provide for you when winter rears its head?

Know the season of life you're in and understand that a season could last a month but it also could last several years. It's not about how long the season lasts; it's about knowing the season you're in, knowing what matters most to you in THIS season and setting goals that can really matter in the current season and will progress well throughout the other three seasons that will eventually come about.

Am I setting at least one goal in each of the four quadrants of life (health, wealth, relationships, spirituality)?

For each of us, there are certain goal areas that feel natural to us… so we have no issue setting goals for that goal arena. But, there are other goal areas (or quadrants) that we resist looking at let alone setting goals for. It's important that you overcome that resistance and make yourself diversify the goals you set. You want your goals to reflect your whole life, not one particular corner of it. In this way, be sure that you're setting at least one goal in each of the four life quadrants:

1. *Health*

    What are your physical, emotional, and psychological health goals? Maybe it's to find a great therapist and get back into weekly therapy. Maybe it's time to drop the last ten pounds and hit your fittest shape ever. Maybe it's time to use a meditation app and get a minimum of 10 minutes of meditation a day. The old saying is true: Health is wealth. Having at least one health goal is a MUST if you want a great shot at living a long, healthy, productive life.

2. *Wealth*

    What are your wealth goals? Do you want to pay off a certain amount of debt? Do you want to increase your income by a certain percentage? Do you want to build a business that earns a certain amount of money each year? Do you want to expand your streams of revenue in your business by adding one or more side hustles to your portfolio? How much money is 'enough' money to fund your lifestyle while giving you plenty of room for savings and play? Do you have a budget? Do you know how much you spend each month? What's your credit score? What's your goal for raising that number? All of these questions could lead to solid wealth goals that will be of great benefit to you in the long run.

3. *Relationships*

How do you want your closest relationships to look? What goals are you setting for your family? Do you want to commit to one evening a week of family time? In terms of couple quality time, do you want to set a goal for a date night every single week? How are your friendships going? Do you feel like you have a great tribe of friends... or would you like to set a goal to intentionally create a high vibing tribe of friends? Again, over your lifespan, relationships NEED to be a priority. What better way to keep connection (and high-quality connection) at the forefront than to set a goal for it?

4. *Spirituality*

Spirituality may not be the best word so replace it with the word that best describes your connection to Spirit, to life, to all that exists that we cannot see with the naked eye. How are you connecting with your soul? How are you practicing stillness? To what extent are you developing self-awareness, mindfulness and the ability to hear from your Inner Knowing? If you practice a religion, to what extent would you like to be involved with that religion? What does that practice look like for you? Answering these questions can lead you down the path of creating a solid goal for developing your spiritual competency.

Please do not apply a perfectionistic approach to setting goals in all four quadrants. I love setting health and wealth goals. I can create them any day of the week but ask me to create a relationship goal and it literally takes me weeks to A- see the value and B- make myself create a goal... and that's okay because I'm working on it.

Notice where you come across resistance to setting a quadrant goal and, rather than beating yourself up for not 'wanting to set the goal', explore the reasons why you feel resistance any time you consider creating a goal for that quadrant. By doing so, you'll learn a lot about yourself and where you have opportunity to grow.

Am I avoiding the most common goal setting traps?

There are many traps that come up when setting goals. I want to cover what I consider the five most common goal setting traps and how you can avoid them.

Goal Setting Trap #1: The Comfort Trap

The Comfort Trap is a goal setting trap where you focus only on the goals you want to pursue. As I talked about in the four quadrants of life, we tend to easily create goals around the topics and in the arenas that we feel most competent in or are most excited by. Because of this bias towards "This is a goal area I like and this feels good to set goals in", we can lean in the direction of setting goals that are 'comfortable' rather than setting goals that we know will require a much heavier (or more boring) lift and will challenge us to grow.

How do you avoid this trap?

Use the quadrants of life to hold yourself accountable to setting at least one goal in each of the life quadrants. More than this, make sure that you're holding yourself as accountable (if not more accountable) to the DMA (Daily Massive Actions) for the less comfortable goals.

In addition, do a 'How important is this goal to my life?' check-in during the goal setting process. Some goals feel super exciting. They have that new car smell but, if we were to ask the question "Will achieving this goal have a massive impact on my life in 5-10 years?", the answer would be 'No.' Don't go after goals because they're exciting in the moment or feel thrilling to pursue. Does it help if a goal is exciting? In the beginning, yes. But, if the goal you're going after isn't a goal that's really going to move the dial on your life, once the honeymoon is over (or once the hard work sets in), you'll drop the goal like it's hot. Don't do that. Make sure the WHY of your goal has a long-lasting impact.

Goal Setting Trap #2: The 'Go For What's Safe' Trap

The 'Go For What's Safe' Trap is a goal setting trap that a lot of people fall into, especially if, in previous months, years and seasons of life they've attempted to go for really big goals and didn't achieve them. The energy that lives behind this trap is an energy that asks "What goal can I set that I know is completely within my realm to achieve and might not challenge me but at least guarantees that I am going to be able to say that I made a commitment to myself and kept it?"

The problem with that kind of thinking is that it's extremely limiting and small in nature. Rather than coming from the place of "What do I need?" or "What do I want?" or "What's meant for me?", the small mindedness of saying "I want to be able to check off the box and say I got it done so what goal can I set that will give me a guarantee that, no matter what goes left in my life, I'm going to be able to accomplish it?" is evident. You can feel the constriction in setting a no brainer goal that doesn't excite, challenge, or grow you... and, yet, people do it because they'd rather check off a box than face the possibility that they might fail at the goal they set. But, the failure in approaching goal setting this way is clear: **You will never grow setting goals that are below your capacity to deliver.**

How do you avoid this trap?

When you set a goal, ask yourself "Is this goal challenging? Will this goal force me to grow? Or is this a goal I could achieve in my sleep? Is this a goal that I feel I have 100% guarantee that, even if life gets crazy, I can still deliver?"

And, if your answer is "Yeah, I know I can accomplish this goal. It's not that hard. I could achieve this in my sleep", either change the goal or level it up to a place where the idea of achieving the goal excites you and scares you at the same time.

Goal Setting Trap #3: The Life Overhaul Trap

The Life Overhaul Trap is a goal setting trap that seems to happen to a lot of people every January 1st. It's this idea of wanting to perform a complete life makeover. We call it "reinvention" but, for many, it's as if they want to run their entire lives through a heavy wash cycle and, seemingly overnight, change everything in their lives.

And here's the problem with that: While having at least one goal in each life quadrant is important, you have to take into consideration the level of effort, the amount of time, and the hours you have available to commit to any and all goals... and then decide if you have enough time and room in your life to pursue those goals at the same time.

The Life Overhaul Trap gets people stuck in a repeat cycle of goal failure because it's not possible to makeover all the big areas of your life at the same time. There is a delicate mix to creating goals that do, over a long period of time, result in a complete life makeover. Yes, you can work on your fitness, your finances, and your relationships at the same but the intensity, complexity, and investment required by each of those goals have to work together with the time you've got available to pursue them. If they don't, you're setting yourself up for failure and for returning to that all-too-familiar limiting belief of "I'm not enough."

How do you avoid this trap?

When you're setting goals, count the cost. Ask yourself "How much time, each week, will this goal require of me?" What will I need to stop doing (and what will I need to start doing) in order to achieve this goal? If I'm going to completely change this area of life, do I really have the energy, strength and time to, at the same time, completely change that area of life?

Answer the questions from a real and raw place... and don't feel bad about the answers you get. If you find that there are two really big areas of life and, from your perspective, both need to change right now, then have both goals but really get to the bones of success on each. What's the bare minimum that needs to happen in order for both goals to get achieved within the timeframe that you set? Drop any other goals that you know, given your focus on both goals, you simply will not have time to pursue.

And remember Pareto's Principle (or the 80/20 rule): 80% of your results comes from 20% of what you do so focus on figuring out which 20% gives you 80% of your results on both goals and laser in on taking those DMAs (Daily Massive Actions).

Goal Setting Trap #4: The Fresh Start Trap

The Fresh Start Trap is a goal setting trap that so many people fall into. It's best described when a person who has a weight loss goal falls short on their healthy eating on a Wednesday and says "Oh well! I'll restart my program on Monday." It's this false notion that a fresh start requires a new day, a new month, a new year, or a new you in order to begin… and here's the reality: You are new in every single moment of your existence. You are not the same today that you were yesterday, the day before that, the week before that, the year before that, or ten years prior to now. We are new in every moment so postponing continuing with a goal or not setting a goal because you want the 'clean slate' feeling of a new year is simply a way to procrastinate becoming who you are meant to be.

How do you avoid this trap?

You can create 'new year, new you' right now. You can restart your goal the second after you fail at taking action on it. You don't have to wait for some arbitrary day or year to have your 'fresh start.' In this way, you avoid the 'Fresh Start' trap by not waiting for a fresh start. Restart the second after you fail. Go for 'New Year, New Me' in every moment. Don't wait for a Monday to get back on your clean eating plan. Start with the very next thing you eat. A shift in your mindset on what a 'fresh start' means is the best way to avoid this trap. A willingness to get right back into goal action is the best way to get out of this trap once you're in it.

Goal Setting Trap #5: The 'Goal Attainment = Happiness' Trap

The 'Goal Attainment = Happiness' Trap is a goal setting trap where you believe that achieving the goal is the key to your happiness. In other words, you say to yourself "When I get this goal, I'll be happy." The unfortunate truth is that if you're not happy on the way to the goal, getting the goal won't make you happy… or it'll thrill you for all of ten seconds when you cross the finish line but leave you in the emptiness of asking "Okay, that was fun. What's next?"

The reason this is a huge goal setting trap is the same reason that thinking you want to leave one partner because the relationship got 'boring' and jump into a new partnership rarely works: the newness eventually wears off. The honeymoon phase ends... and so much of life is the process of getting to goals that, if you really think that, upon achieving a goal, all of your life should now shift from what it was to this golden dream of happiness, you're going to be very, very disappointed.

You see, life is about the process of becoming great, not the greatness itself. And we live with the reality that all of life is this wonderful adventure of rises and falls. Some years are good. Some years are awful. Some things work out well. Other things really suck... and we have no crystal ball to tell us which will be which... and the people who learn how to fall in love with the process of getting to their goals (rather than having a false expectation that their lives will suddenly morph once they achieve them) do far better, in terms of happiness, than those who live in the fantasy that, once the goal is achieved, their entire lives will change for the better.

How do you avoid this trap?

When setting goals, do not set goals that feel like they are the 'rescuers' of your life. Remind yourself that happiness is ALWAYS an inside job, that you can choose to be happy in any moment you're in and that most of your life will be spent on the journey to the next goal. Refocus your attention and ask "How can I fall in love with the in-between, with the journey to the goal? How can I get real with how little time I'll actually ever spend in the bliss of achieving any one goal and, instead, find joy in the ordinary moments and in the everyday doing and being of my life?"

If you can keep your perspective there, you'll make it a lifetime goal to figure out how to fall in love with the process of becoming great and that's the key to happiness. You might have amazing goals but, if you're only going to choose to be happy once you achieve them, how much of your life are you also choosing to be unhappy? Oh yeah... most of it. Don't do that...

Do I TRUST my goal setting approach?

Now that we've talked through Maslow's Hierarchy of Needs, the seasons of life, and goal setting traps, I'd like to share my goal setting process with you. I call it the TRUST process of goal setting.

Before we dive into it, let me make a few disclaimers:

> ➤ I am a VERY detailed oriented person; one of my top love languages is spreadsheets and I live my life by checking off boxes in those spreadsheets so what you're about to learn reflects that orientation

> ➤ Because this is a detail oriented approach, it does require a considerable amount of time, much more time than a more generalist "Write down your goals every day" approach would take; I do have shortened versions of daily goal writing that I use when I am short on time but I find that the more intentional I am about taking the time do review, assess and write down my goals, the higher the chances of those goals getting achieved

> ➤ TRUST is one of many goal setting techniques that exist in the world and it may not resonate with you... and that's okay. The main takeaway I'd like you to get out of this chapter is not that my technique is the ONLY one that works but that you need a goal setting technique that you subscribe to and use as your goal setting system for EVERY goal you set. Find the goal setting technique that feels right for you and then implement it with vigilant consistency; that's the point of this chapter

The TRUST Goal Setting Method

When I approach the art and science of goal setting, I focus on TRUST:

➢ **T**op 10 goals

➢ **R**everse engineer the decade

➢ **U**nderstand the 3 Cs (capacity, commitment and criteria for success)

➢ **S**eparate into milestones, months, weeks, days and focus blocks

➢ **T**ake DMA (Daily Massive Action)

Let's dive into each of the five goal setting steps…

Step #1: Top 10 Goals

In Chapter 2, we talked about your top 10 life goals. Refer back to that list. In the TRUST goal setting process, we begin with those top ten goals. Why? Because, far too often, if we focus only on what we want for this year or for the next three years, we end up focusing on objectives that, in the grand scheme of our lives, doesn't end up being a huge priority.

By listing your top 10 goals, you now move into Step #2 focused on what lower order goals need to get achieved to make the fulfillment of those top 10 goals possible. You also go into the remaining goal setting steps with a long-game mindset. You're no longer looking at things from the perspective of "What do I want this year?" Instead, you're saying to yourself "If I'm going to get where I want to be in the next ten years, what are the key milestones that will lead me to the exact outcomes I want in the next decade?"

Write out your top ten life goals and, for each of those goals, put a goal due date. It's important for Step #2 that you have a solid idea of when you'd like to see each of those ten life goals achieved.

Step #2: Reverse engineer the decade

Once you have your top ten life goals, it's time to reverse engineer the decade. We want to begin by asking the question "Given my top ten life goals, where do I want to be in ten years' time?" We also want to ask "Which of my top ten life goals do I anticipate achieving in the next ten years?" Those goals then become your decade goals.

In this way, we start with a vision of our Future Selves and map all of the steps our Future Self took to get from that point in ten years until we arrive today.

There are a few reasons for this:
- ✓ To properly set goals for this year, I have to have an idea of what I want to have achieved in ten years; every goal I set and achieve this year needs to be leading me to the bigger goals I'd like to have achieved by the time I've completed the next ten years of my life.
- ✓ I want to be sure that I'm not overestimating what I can do in a year and underestimating what I can accomplish in a decade; unless I've reverse engineered the decade (i.e. mapping my 10 years-from-now life to today), I won't have a clear sense of whether the goals I'm setting for this year actually need to be two to three year goals, not one.
- ✓ If I'm not taking AT LEAST one step EVERY SINGLE DAY towards my decade goals, then something about my action taking system or my goal management process is off... and I want to catch that before I spend too many weeks or months in an unhelpful pattern of moving forward.

It's important to keep in mind that it may take you a few days to a few weeks to sit down and map out your decade. That's fine. But, be clear with yourself and don't take any more time than is needed to complete this step in the goal setting process. Sometimes, procrastination comes in the form of spending too much time planning.

Step #3: Understand the 3 Cs *(capacity, commitment and criteria for success)*
One of the things that can make goal setting feel like a very daunting task comes when you feel like there's so much you want to accomplish and so little time within which to accomplish those things. This is where Step #3 in the TRUST goal setting process comes in. I like to think of this step as the "Let's get real" step of the process.

Understanding the 3 Cs involves assessing the following:
- ✓ *Capacity-* How much time, energy, money and support will achieving your decade goals require? DISCLAIMER: 99.9% of the time, we're going to drastically underestimate the capacity that will be required to actually get to our goals; the point isn't to be 100% accurate on the capacity answer right now; the point is to get a ballpark sense of what capacity you'll need for the journey so you can decide, before finalizing the goals, whether you're willing to stretch and deliver that level of capacity
- ✓ *Commitment-* How committed are you to achieving these goals? Meaning… if your goals required three times the amount of energy, effort and time to achieve while also requiring that you give up certain activities and focuses that you now have in your life AND you needed to do that for several years (5-7 years), would you still be whole-heartedly committed to this goal? Would you still be ALL IN?
- ✓ *Criteria-* So often, I see people wanting to set what they're calling 'doable' goals but what I can see are goals that are far below what they're capable of achieving… all in the name of ensuring 100% guarantee that they can and will achieve the goal. The problem with this comes when you set goals that are below you and, in doing so, create criteria for success that doesn't mean anything to you in the long run. You end up approaching those goals with half ass effort and half ass interest. In this way, your criteria for success doesn't feel successful… and then you walk around feeling the shame that comes with 'gaming the goal system', all to say "I achieved the goal." In this sense, establishing your criteria of success is an assessment of 1- defining what done looks like for each of your goals and 2- deciding if your definition of done

actually feels like success to you. Unless you can meet both criteria (i.e. "I know what done looks like on this goal" and "Done feels like I've gone above and beyond, challenged myself, and have had to put in a high level of performance to get to this goal"), you don't have solid criteria for success. What you have is a checklist and a checklist will not motivate you to stay the course when the going gets tough.

Step #4: Separate into milestones, months, weeks, days and focus blocks

Here's where the detail work in the TRUST goal setting process comes in. Once you have your top 10 life goals and your decade goals (oftentimes, they're one in the same), it's time to break those goals down even further. We want to take the decade goals and break them down into the following components:

➢ Decade goals
➢ Yearly goals
➢ Quarterly goals
➢ Monthly goals
➢ Weekly goals
➢ Daily goals

Let me start by confronting an immediate fear that comes up with Step #4, a fear that still comes up for me every time I do goal setting... and it's this:

Where do I even start with mapping out the decade, yearly, quarterly, monthly, weekly and daily goals for EACH of my goals? The idea alone is so overwhelming!!!!!!!!

First, to combat that immediate sense of dread and overwhelm, we need to make this process creative and fun. Get colored pencils and big paper. Use pencil to write these things in (or erasable pen) so you can easily change things as you're doing this. Create enough space and room on your desk so that you can sit with this process and have plenty of room to think, draw, write and room for your supplies. We start with creativity and fun which will reduce some of the overwhelm.

Second, as you're taking the time to break down each goal into decade, yearly, quarterly, monthly, weekly and daily goals, keep a journal close and reflect on the question "How can I bring ten years from now into today? What 7-day experiments can I try to bring some of my 10-years-from-now life into today, this week, this year?" Jot those ideas down.

From there, you're going to want to spend the time to create a goal pyramid for each of your decade long goals and then break each goal down into its component parts. Once you do that, you want to take the goals for the year from each decade goal and evaluate whether you can accomplish all of those things this year. You may need to refine decade goals to ensure that the goals you're working on for this year are realistic to achieve so you achieve all of the goals you've listed in 10 years.

Once you've broken down all of your decade goals, store the planning for everything but the yearlong goals in a folder. Now zone in on this year's goals and break them down into monthly and weekly goals. Once you've done that, find a way to keep your monthly and weekly goals somewhere you can see them every single day. Design your DMAs (Daily Massive Actions) based on what needs to happen by the end of the week.

Step #5: Take DMA *(Daily Massive Action)*
Your Daily Massive Actions are the actions you take, on a daily basis, to achieve your weekly, monthly, yearly and decade long goals. Your DMAs are not decided arbitrarily and need to be deliverables that have clear metrics of success. For example, if your yearlong goal is to write a 120,000 word book, that would break down to you needing to write 10,000 words per month which then breaks down to 2,500 words per week which then breaks down to writing approximately 360 words per day. One of your DMAs, then, would be to write 360 words of your book every single day.

While your Daily Massive Actions (DMAs) might not always be that clearcut, you want to come as close as you possibly can to a daily success list of actions you need to take so you move through each day operating on purpose. List out the phone calls you need to make, the emails you need to send, how many pages of a book you need to read, the number of job applications you need to put in. Get clear on what and how much you need to do in a given day and you've got solid DMAs (Daily Massive Actions).

The key to successfully and consistently taking Daily Massive Action is your schedule. Tony Robbins put it best when he said "If it's not scheduled, it's not real." If your goal is to lose twenty-four pounds in the next six months (24 weeks), that breaks down to losing one pound a week. One pound a week breaks down to you decreasing your caloric intake (or burning calories through exercise) in the amount of 3,500 calories. Now that we have the metric of success, you can figure out how much cardio and how many calories you need to burn off and take in each day to ensure that you hit your one pound of weight loss each week.

To follow through, you've got to schedule your exercise times on your calendar AND stick to them. Arbitrarily saying "I'll burn 300 calories a day and figure out when I'm going to do that as I go through each day" is your fastest way to failure. The same way you would schedule an appointment to talk to an accountant or a personal trainer, you need to put your Daily Massive Action focus blocks on your calendar because those are the most important appointments of your life… and they should be treated with the corresponding level of respect and commitment.

At the end of the day, so much of what I've walked you through in this chapter is ABSOLUTELY BORING. It's not all that fun or sexy to have to break down goals into their nitty gritty parts. While I am detailed oriented, I find doing this process a complete and total drag… and, yet, it's still got to get done… and the power in doing it is clear.

Once I have my year mapped out down to weekly goals, when I wake up every day, I'm no longer asking myself "What am I supposed to be doing today?" Instead, I pull out the binder with my plan where I've placed my weekly goals and breakdown of the daily massive actions needed THIS week to get there and I spend fifteen minutes planning the day. The only question I'm asking at this point is "Where, on today's calendar, am I dedicating the time to get the DMAs done that need to get done if I'm going to achieve my weekly goals?" It makes life so simple! I'm no longer focused on the bigger picture. I don't have to keep the decade goals in mind. I can put WHOLE mind into PRESENT action because I've already mapped out what it's going to take to get to the 10-years-from-now me.

And that's the point of any goal setting system: to give you a simple, straight forward way to identify what you want, how to get it, and what you'll need to invest today to give you your best shot at achievement. Take the time to use the TRUST process and, once you've completed it, the only thing you'll need to do, from that point to the victory line, is work. Get to it...

CHAPTER 11: HOW TO ORGANIZE YOUR LIFE FOR GOAL ACHIEVEMENT

Your past does not have to keep repeating itself. If you don't like how the future looks, change it."
- Unknown

Have you ever observed a person who seemingly flows from one level of success to another? I'm not talking about a celebrity or social media star or even one of your family members who's only posting the 'good parts' on social. I'm talking about someone you know in real life who seems to easily decide what they want, develop a plan, take action and get exactly what they want and does this no matter how big the goal is.

Do you know someone like that?

Chances are, you do. You might wonder "How does that person achieve goals seemingly effortlessly and I'm finding it so hard to get a little bit of progress in?" The answer to that question is the topic of this chapter… and it's not going to feel great to get real with the differences between what that person is doing and what you're currently allowing… and it's necessary.

It all comes down to the vast difference between how that person (that you know) sets up their life versus how you organize your life for goal achievement. When I say 'organize your life for goal achievement', I'm talking about a variety of life factors, including:
- ➢ Where you live
- ➢ How much debt you've taken on (and now have to repay)
- ➢ The number of children you've chosen to raise (including 'adults' who you are taking responsibility for)
- ➢ The partner you've chosen
- ➢ How you eat (which impacts your health and energy)
- ➢ How often you move (which impacts your health and energy)
- ➢ How you think about life (your mindset)
- ➢ The narrative you tell yourself about your life (victim or victor)

- ➢ What you consistently focus on (what IS working or what ISN'T working?)
- ➢ Who you spend the most time with (your tribe of people- are they lifting you up or bringing you down?)
- ➢ Your habits, both good and bad
- ➢ Your sleep
- ➢ The state of clutter in your home
- ➢ Your spirituality
- ➢ Your connection with your own soul
- ➢ Your chosen profession or career (and how much harder you work for others than you do for yourself)

I could go on and on but you get my drift…

Very often, the people we know in life who are moving from one level of success to the other with ease are doing so because they've intentionally created a life environment that makes achieving their goals the easiest it possibly can be. Now… nothing about achieving big goals is easy… for anyone. However, you can make it harder to move your life from one level to the next the more you add difficult or complex environmental factors to it.

If you're reading this and you're saying to yourself "Well great! Then I'm screwed!", keep reading. Yes, your journey might be more difficult, and you may have a lot of course correction, adjustment, and organizational shifting to do but you still can create an environment that is far more conducive to achieving your goals than the one you're currently living in. You can change things, but you've got to get clear on what needs to change and then take the steps necessary to change them… which leads us to a discussion of the size of your dreams.

How do you feel about the size of your dreams? Do they feel too big? To small? Just right? More importantly, have you ever feared the size of your dream or the perceived immense gap between where you are right now and where you want to be?

A lot of people feel a tremendous amount of fear when it comes to pursuing their biggest goals and dreams. They think the fear is about the size of the dream when, in fact, the fear is about a subtle knowing that they lack the right environment in which to pursue and achieve those goals. There's clarity around what they want but a fuzziness around operating in a way that's conducive to having what they want.

While the goal is clear, the best approach to achieving the goal is not... and the current environment in which they work and live feels off. It feels NOT conducive to the level of focus and performance they know they're going to need to achieve the goals. More than that, in some cases, their environment feels antagonistic to what they're going for so there's this constant sense of having to 'fight' to get in the time or the focus they need on goals, as if their environment is working against their best interest... and the problem is not the environment itself; the problem is the way they've allowed the environment to dictate their limits rather than creating an environment built to encourage their success.

When the road to your goals feels like pushing a boulder uphill, on some level, you have bypassed a very important goal achievement step: organizing your life in such a way that the achievement of the goal, no matter what happens next, becomes unassailable because the environment you take action in was built to make you unstoppable.

You might be saying to yourself "Okay, I haven't intentionally created my action taking environment and this environment does feel like I'm fighting against it to get stuff done. How do I change this?" The answer is simple but not easy. **You need to rebuild your environment.**

When it comes to setting up your goal achievement environment, you want to create an environment that allows you to be what Sun Tzu, in <u>The Art of War</u>, describes as "Swift as the wind, quiet as the forest, conquer like the fire, steady as the mountain."

What do each of those elements mean?

➢ *Swift as the wind:* How can you set up your environment so you're able to be efficient, productive and get right to work on achieving your goals? How can you take decisive action quickly and keep an eye on the effectiveness of your strategies so that, the moment you see a strategy isn't working, you can easily pivot and do something else?

➢ *Quiet as the forest:* Rather than making pronunciations about all the things you're going to do, rather than spending more time talking about your goals than working on them, what if you conserved all of that "I'm telling the world what I'm up to!" energy and channel that into getting things done? Anthony Trucks calls it working in the dark. You never have to speak about your results. Do the work and let the results speak for themselves.

➢ *Conquer like the fire:* If you're going to go after a goal, make sure you're going after EVERTHING you want. Small goals bring small energy with them. What is it that you REALLY want? Not what you 'think' you can have but the BIG thing that's so intriguing to you that, by going for that, you feel compelled to jump out of bed and take action on it? Go after that thing and then keep going after big things, not simply because you want them but because you know you can achieve them. A Sun Tzu quote describes this best: "Opportunities multiply as they are seized." The more opportunities you go after AND get, the more abundant you feel, the more confident you get and the easier both seeing and seizing opportunities starts to become.

➢ *Steady as the mountain:* You have to be sold on the fact that your goal is ALREADY DONE, that it's inevitable, that you ARE doing this, that there's no Plan B, that you are ALL IN and that you will be the last person standing. When you get 100% clear on that, the obstacles no longer shake you. You know life storms will come and you know that you will stand as steady as the mountain against them because your end goal is clear... and you aren't leaving until you get where you say you want to be.

I've given you the ballpark definition of what each of those elements mean. At the end of the day, only you know what gets you all of those elements. **Here's what's clear: if you want to have your goal achievement feel more like flow than force, you have to find a way to that.**

Is your 'swift as the wind' having your laptop set up, water bottle on your desk and clothes laid out so getting to work is as simple as waking up? Is your 'quiet as the forest' working in the dark, not telling anyone about your goals, and achieving them quietly? Is your 'Conquer the fire' going ALL IN on your goal, staying up late, waking up early, working weekends, giving everything you've got to this ONE thing? Is your 'Steady as the mountain' being able to take the losses, the setbacks, the obstacles and, even when you feel like giving up, getting up and immediately getting back to work? Only you can answer that...

Here's what's not negotiable: Creating an environment that is prepped and ready to go before you engage in the work of goal achievement. If you want to be your most productive self, this is a must.

"Victorious warriors win first and then go to war, while defeated warriors go to war first and then seek to win." – Sun Tzu

To successfully prepare your environment for taking DMA (Daily Massive Action), begin by assessing the current setup of the different 'homes' you live in.

In general, we live in seven homes throughout our lives:

1. **Physical Home:** This represents the place you actually live- your apartment, flat, townhome, house, condo, or estate. It's not simply the actual structure but also the way you've set up that physical structure. Do you like the way your furniture is laid out? Do you like how your home smells and looks? How much clutter do you have in your house? Does your home feel open and abundant from an energy perspective?

2. **Body Home:** A powerful quote states "You can never truly feel at home in a body that you view as temporary." Your body home is the physiological home that is your body. It's the health and vitality (or the illness and lack of energy) that you're currently

fostering in your body that will factor into how much energy and focus you're able to give to your goals.

3. **Emotional Home:** Your emotional home represents where you typically live emotionally. Do you feel emotionally centered? Do you have that ability to feel emotions and allow them to move through you? Do you veer in the direction of spending more time in a negative emotion state... or in a positive one? Your emotional calibration can be changed but you've first got to know where you tend to live on an emotional level. Emotional mastery requires emotional calibration. Your emotions are going to shift in all sorts of ways as you pursue your goals. Given that, your life has to be well organized so that, when your mind or emotions go rogue, you still have a plan to follow, and you hold your actions to the plan while you get your mind and heart back in check. It goes back to staying focused on the important things. As a powerful quote says, "Don't let something that doesn't matter make you lose something that does."

4. **Energetic Home:** Each person comes into this life with a unique energy. There's a vibe to every person. Some people are super fiery; other people have energy that feels very calm and centered. What is your natural energetic position, and do you feel full of that energy on a regular basis? Or... do you feel energetically drained most of the time? That's the place that your energetic home is currently operating from.

5. **Spiritual Home:** How do you connect with your soul on a regular basis? How connected do you feel to your Inner Knowing? How much do you trust and listen to your intuition? How much time do you spend in stillness, listening for the messages from your soul? The answers to those questions point to the quality of your spiritual home. A wonderful quote says "The body benefits from movement and the mind benefits from stillness."

6. **Relational Home:** Your relational home, first and foremost, is about the relationship you have with yourself. Do you like who you are? Do you give yourself your undivided attention? Do you feel good about you? Liking yourself is a bare minimum requirement to being able to take action on your goals and dreams. If you are at war with yourself, you have no bandwidth of energy

or focus to make an unequivocal decision. If you lack the ability to decide, you lack the capacity to move forward. That's a big problem when it comes to goal achievement. Your relational home is also about the people closest to you. Who's your love? What's your family like? How are your closest friends? Do they hold space for you… or do they make you feel unsafe? Your answers will tell you the quality of your relational home.

7. **Geographic Home:** Your geographic home is the country, state, city and neighborhood you live. Do you live where you feel most at home? You automatically know the answer to that. If the answer is No, guess what? You need to make a plan and find a way to move to wherever home is for you. You'll know it once you arrive there.

Once you have a pulse on where all seven 'homes' are, it's time to ask yourself some important questions about what needs to change in each of those areas. Take thirty minutes to ask and answer the following questions:

➢ What about this home is working?
➢ What about this home needs to change?
➢ What's my plan for changing it?
➢ How will I hold myself accountable?
➢ What's my first step and when will I take that step?

And let me be VERY clear- I'm not saying all seven homes need to be in perfect alignment for you to achieve your goals. There are many people whose entire lives are a hot mess and they still get goals achieved. But, could they have gotten to their goals faster and could they have taken their lives farther if they weren't fighting multiple battles on different fronts ALL OF THE TIME? Of course! Save yourself a loss of time and energy by cleaning up as much of your environment (i.e. your homes) as you can.

What if you're reading this and saying to yourself "Kassandra, this all sounds fine and good but, right now, my life is a hot mess. My home life is horrible. I'm surrounded by toxic people. I want to get a divorce but can't afford to do it. No one in my life supports my goals or dreams. I'm so stressed all of the time. I'm operating on very little sleep. I never feel ease. My health is deteriorating. I'm at my wit's end and, while I get what you're saying about making sure all of my 'homes' are good, I don't have the capacity to do any of that right now. I am barely keeping my head above water. So... how can this help me at all?"

First of all, I've been in that situation more than once. I've been in seasons of my life where I felt emotionally, physically, spiritually and financially exhausted, where I felt like no matter how hard I worked and tried to change things, nothing was moving. In those seasons of my life, I felt stuck, angry that I was stuck, completely unsupported, and absolutely unworthy.

And here's what those seasons taught me: Nothing was going to change until I got VERY honest about what wasn't working in my life, VERY clear about what MUST change in my life NOW (even if I didn't know how the hell I was going to change it), and ENTIRELY FOCUSED on taking the steps required to change those pieces with a TRUE sense of urgency.

Let me give you an example.

There have been several times in my life when I've found myself living in a state, town or home that I haven't liked, felt was absolutely not right for me and I spent YEARS living in that space. I was miserable to the point where my health deteriorated, my happiness went away, and I felt sapped of all energy. Yes, I was taking action every single day on my goals while living in those places but it took everything I had to make a tiny bit of progress. I was not firing on all cylinders and my action taking had a deep sense of unworthiness behind it. I was struggling to take action to get out of a situation that I wasn't willing to address now in the hopes that 'later' would come soon... it didn't.

So, in every season where I've had this happen, one thing occurs: I hit a breaking point. I can't explain what caused the breaking point or what led to me finally saying "Enough is enough!" but I get to this point where the pain is so high and the cost has become so much that I finally say "I cannot delay changing this anymore!" At that point, my Higher Self won't allow me to ignore the game changing moves that need to be made. I get to this point where I'm willing to surrender whatever has to be surrendered, to let go of whatever (or whoever) needs to be let go of JUST so I can have peace… and then I start ushering people, situations and toxic elements out of my life like there's no tomorrow.

And it's unfortunate that it took me getting to my breaking point to do that. Tony Robbins talks about the fact that we're more motivated by pain than we are by pleasure and I don't love that it's true… and, yet, it is.

If you're reading this and you haven't yet hit your breaking point, here's my advice: Act as if you're at your breaking point and start taking the actions now. Here's my other piece of advice: If you can't get yourself to do that, leave it alone. Your breaking point will come soon enough.

I wish I could give you some model or strategy that would make what I've just said not so. I wish I could tell you that you can live in a chaotic house full of super toxic people and you can achieve all of your goals and dreams in the time and fashion that you would achieve them if those toxic elements were not in place. Alas, I cannot say that because it simply isn't true. We are energetic beings and, because we are brimming with energy every moment of every day, nobody's neutral. Every person you come in contact with will impact your energy and you will impact theirs. To say otherwise would be to set yourself up to be very, very disappointed by life.

At the end of the day, your best goal achievement environment will be one that feels open, spacious and energizing. To create such an environment, you will need to shift a lot of things- the thoughts you think, the choices you make, the things you do or don't do, who you hang out with, even down to the way you organize the rooms in your home and how clear the space on your desk is. It's all significant and it all matters.

But, you'll also need to address the elephants in the room that you keep trying to avoid:
- The relationships that are unsupportive and draining
- The people pleasing tendencies that keep you avoiding your own life

- The pull you feel to shiny objects and what's 'new' and exciting rather than mastering boredom and staying the course on your biggest goals
- The difficult conversations you need to have around boundaries and honoring what the time you need to work on your goals
- The clutter that's taking up space in your house and clogging your mind so you're not able to be as creative and productive as you want to be
- Your lack of consistency in having a daily routine that works for you and the excuses you make about why you don't stick to one
- Your tendency to take on people as projects... and the significant price you pay for trying to fix people you didn't break
- You putting so much time and energy into helping people achieve their goals when you are out of integrity with yours

These are not easy issues to tackle but they must be handled if your environment is going to be conducive to success... and the emotional/energetic issues of your life MUST be handled as you work through the logistical/setup dilemmas of your goal achievement environment. Both have to be handled.

It's one thing for me to tell you "Make sure your laptop is set up and ready to go in the morning. Keep only the web tabs open that you need. Have your clothes and water bottle ready to go." Its quite another thing for me to tell you "Sit your family down and explain to them how many hours a week you need to be left alone in your home office. Go further into explaining to them that, if your boundaries aren't honored, you're going to start to work at Starbucks and you will turn off your phone." That conversation is not an easy one to have but a necessary one to engage in.

At the end of the day, your environment can build you up or it can keep you feeling down. Do your best to control the elements in it that you can control. Make sure that both the physical and energetic aspects of your environment feel healthy, safe, and energizing FOR YOU... And what that requires will be different for each person. You KNOW what you need. Make sure that you do what is required to get it. Organize your life in such a way that taking action feels way more like flex and flow than it does like pushing a boulder uphill.

Remember: Nobody's going to change your environment for you. You know what you need. Give it to yourself...

CHAPTER 12: GOAL MANAGEMENT DOS AND DON'TS

If I waited until I had all my ducks in a row,
I'd never get across the street.
Sometimes you just have to gather up
what you've got and make a run for it.
- Anonymous

I have a love hate relationship with the idea of taking bi-weekly progress pics, weight and inches measurements on my fitness journey. Having once been a personal trainer and in phenomenal shape, I understand the power of seeing your body transform through pictures over time. I also get the importance of being able to compare measurements from one two-week period to the next over three to six months. Having that data allows a person to get clear on what strategies are working and what strategies are not.

But, here's where, as I embark upon a new fitness challenge that's going to take me two to three years to complete, where I struggle: Bi-weekly measurements won't tell me anything that my daily goal management activities haven't already told me. For example, I know what my daily calories need to be and have my macros down to the percentage of fat, protein, and carbs I'm supposed to get in daily. If I miss the mark on five to seven days of this week, guess what? I'm not hitting my two-pound weight loss goal for this week. I don't have to step on a scale or take progress pics. The lead measure that asks "Are you sticking to your macros today?" gives me the answer that's going to get confirmed when I step on the scale on Sunday.

The same thing applies to my cardio and weightlifting. I have a workout calendar that indicates the exact types and duration of exercise I'm supposed to be doing each day of the week. If I miss four out of seven days or if I only do half of what's on the workout calendar, I don't need a progress pic to show me that there's little to no progress. The lead measure of my workout calendar tells me everything I need to know.

And herein lies the power of goal management. When done correctly, every single day you know whether you are on or off track to reach each of your goals. It is the science behind the art of goal setting and, while most people love to set goals, most people hate to do the goal management piece. It's analytical, tedious and it will call you out on the truth of why you're not getting where you want to be as fast as you could be getting there.

Goal management is an unsexy process that must be done. It's about knowing the details and the markers of your success and holding yourself accountable to those markers day in and day out. It's about taking a daily, weekly and monthly pulse on how you're doing with your goals.

There are five components to goal management:
1. Breaking down your goals into key milestones and monthly, weekly and daily deliverables
2. Scheduling focus blocks that are attached to completing specific deliverables.
3. A physical scorecard that can be checked off every single day to ensure that each day's deliverables are complete.
4. Monthly, daily and weekly goal review to assess what's going well, what's not going well and what needs to change
5. Scheduled rest time in between push periods of goal achievement

Let's walk through each of the five components in more detail...

#1: Break down your goals into key milestones and monthly, weekly and daily deliverables.
Pull out your goals for the next twelve month. For each goal, identify the following:
- ✓ Goal achievement date
- ✓ Key milestones
- ✓ Yearly goals
- ✓ Quarterly goals
- ✓ Monthly goals
- ✓ Weekly goals
- ✓ Daily Massive Actions

Take a closer look at this month's goals. What has to be accomplished each week to get to the month's goals? Approximately how long do you think it will take to achieve each of the weekly goals? Write down the weekly goals and the amount of time you think it will take out of this week to accomplish each of those goals.

#2: Schedule focus blocks that are attached to completing specific deliverables.

Decide how you'll set up this week's focus blocks to get in enough time (plus some wiggle room) to accomplish this week's goals. Schedule those focus blocks on your calendar. Build in 5-10 minutes of transition time into the front and back end of each focus block (i.e. add 10 – 20 minutes to each focus block so you take into consideration the amount of time required to context switch from one area of focus to another). Be sure that you schedule focus blocks to accomplish your most challenging tasks as early in the day as possible.

The logic behind this is best expressed by Gary Keller in The ONE Thing. He refers to an article written by Paul Graham in 2009. In this article, Keller says that Graham "divides all work into two buckets: maker (do or create) and manager (oversee or direct). "Maker" time requires large blocks of the clock to write code, develop ideas, generate leads, recruit people, produce products, or execute on projects and plans."

Keller goes on to say "'Manager time', on the other hand, gets divided into hours. This time typically has one moving from meeting to meeting, and because those who oversee or direct tend to have power and authority, "they are in a position to make everyone resonate at their frequency."

And here's Keller's wisdom about this: "To experience extraordinary results, be a maker in the morning and a manager in the afternoon."

Time blocking your DMAs (Daily Massive Actions) is the best way to ensure that you're allocating the time you need to get your weekly, monthly and yearly goals achieved.

#3: Create a physical scorecard that can be checked off every single day to ensure that each day's deliverables are complete.

Cal Newport, in Deep Work, calls this a compelling scorecard. In <u>Deep Work</u>, he quotes the authors of 4DX and says "People play differently when they're keeping score." There's power in having a big annual calendar hanging on your wall next to your desk. On that calendar, you want to list the deliverables you've scheduled focus blocks for every day of the week. As you meet your DMA goals and achieve those deliverables, put an X over that day on the calendar. The goal is to get 7 Xs in a row each week. You'd be surprised how motivating it is to see weeks of consecutive Xs checked off. You know you're on pace to achieve your bigger goals.

#4: Schedule (and keep) a daily, weekly and monthly goal review appointment with yourself.

I spend the first 15-30 minutes and the last 15-30 minutes of each workday assessing progress on my goals. I then consider my start-up and shut-down business rituals. This dedicated time is used to ask myself a number of important questions.

In the morning, my business start-up ritual involves looking at progress (or lack thereof) and asking myself:

➢ What's working in my business strategy?
➢ What's not working in my business strategy?
➢ How on pace am I to achieve this month's business goals?
➢ If I'm delayed or behind, what do I need to shift to either catch up or adjust the monthly goals?
➢ How can I put my business focus blocks in periods of the day that are better suited to productivity than they currently are?
➢ What else is missing from my approach?
➢ What else needs to change?

In the evening, before I shut down my laptop for the night, I review what got done during the day and I assess the effectiveness of the way I set up today's focus blocks.

I ask myself the following questions each night:
➢ What worked about the way I approached DMA?

➤ What didn't work?
➤ What will I do differently tomorrow?

#5: Schedule rest time in between push periods of goal achievement.

Here's where it becomes important to have your yearly goals broken down into quarterly, monthly, and weekly goals. Once you have a good sense of what you plan to accomplish in twelve months' time, it's critical that you schedule rest time in between push periods.

Gary Keller describes it this way in <u>The ONE Thing</u>:
"To achieve extraordinary results and experience greatness, time block these three things in the following order: 1 – Time block your time off, 2 – Time block your ONE Thing, and 3 – Time block your planning time." He goes on to say "When you intend to be successful, you start by protecting time to recharge and reward yourself… Resting is as important as working."

Whether it is a day of rest each week, a weekend getaway each quarter or three week long vacations a year, before you fully map out all of your focus blocks for the year, put your vacation/rest time on your calendar FIRST… and then build your work schedule around your rest calendar (and not the other way around).

Now that you understand how to do goal management, let's talk about a few goal management Dos and Don'ts.

Goal Management Dos:

✓ **Do be hypervigilant about tracking your daily progress.**
Even on days when you know you're not getting enough done, still track and assess what went well and what didn't go well.

✓ **Do give yourself two to four dedicated weekends in October or November** (avoid December due to the holidays and family gatherings that usually take up most of your time) **to plan out next year's milestones and associated monthly, weekly and daily goals.** If it works better, schedule an entire week in October, go to a nurturing, beautiful place away from home and enjoy a week away focused on one thing- the next year's goals. It'll be both a treat and a task.

- ✓ **Do keep your focus on what's working** and your ability to change whatever is not working.
- ✓ **Do put more focus on getting the deliverable done than on the number of hours you're putting into working on the deliverable.** Hours matter very little if the deliverable doesn't get done. Focus on done and give to the deliverable whatever hours are required to get there.
- ✓ **Do see goal management as one large experiment.** It's going to take you time to improve your accuracy about how long you think things will take to complete. Expect to be wrong about that a lot… at first. Keep track of your estimations versus how much time things actually took. You'll become more accurate over time. Be patient with the process.
- ✓ **Do get your most important deliverable done as early in the day as you can.** This decreases the likelihood that life (or other people) will get in the way.

Goal Management Don'ts:

- ✓ **Don't publicize every action you're taking on your goals.** A- It's using time that could be spent taking DMA (Daily Massive Action) and B- Seeking goal achievement praise before you've achieved the goal diminishes your sense of urgency to actually get to the goal.
- ✓ **Don't look for shortcuts or fast ways to get your goals done.** Oftentimes, the 'shortcuts' produce massive delays or needs for rework that, at the end of the day, wind up taking more time than you would've used doing things in their proper order.
- ✓ **Don't see saw between various DMAs (Daily Massive Actions).** When you get up in the morning (or the night before), select your DMAs and stick to them. Constantly changing what you expect to achieve each day creates a lack of focus, a ton of indecision and, before you know it, you're stuck in analysis paralysis getting nothing accomplished.
- ✓ **Don't ignore what your intuition is telling you to focus on next.** In most cases, if your intuition tells you to focus on a particular thing, it's right. Listen to your intuition and follow through on the next action it tells you to take.

Goal management can be very mundane and boring. The secret to goal achievement on any level comes with the need to master boredom. See goal management as your opportunity to do so. Even if you feel like you're a person who's not good at managing details, there are a few things I want you to remember so you KNOW how important it is that you do this step:

➢ The goals you make are a promise you are making to yourself... and you are not a person who breaks promises.

➢ You have promised yourself a certain quality of life and lifestyle; it is up to you to follow through on that promise.

➢ There is no such thing as giving up on your dreams. "Champions keep playing until they get it right." – Unknown

➢ Your life is up to you and no one can take over the management of your life for you but you. Own your power and your responsibility to successfully manage your goals and your life.

➢ There is no promised or guaranteed path to achieving your goals. "We learn the way on the way." – Unknown

➢ To achieve your biggest goals and dreams, you're going to have to learn to say No without guilt and Yes without fear. Getting good at goal management is one of the fastest ways to do that.

Final Point: You are worth whatever it takes to achieve your goals. Put another way, someone (I'm not sure who) once said "The price we pay for being ourselves is worth it."

You are worth it. Teach yourself to manage your goals well...

CHAPTER 13: WHEN TO GOAL SHIFT... AND WHEN TO STAY THE COURSE

If you don't risk anything,
you risk even more.
- Erica Jong

In my mid-twenties, I really wanted to go to law school. Well, what it really boiled down to was I really wanted to go to Georgetown Law School. I studied for the LSAT (half-ass studied for it), scored okay (but not within Georgetown's range), applied to Georgetown and other law schools... and got waitlisted at Georgetown. You can imagine how quickly the desire to achieve the goal of 'become a lawyer' left me once I didn't get into Georgetown... which proved to me that the goal I spent over a year working on was a goal I should've never pursued in the first place.

Why?

Because I didn't really want to be a lawyer. I wanted to go to Georgetown... and that was not a reason to invest a year of my life into something that I really didn't want.

This is why it's important to know when it's time to goal shift. A lot of this book has been spent talking about the power of staying the course, the persistence and grit required to achieve your biggest dreams, and why it's critical to apply tunnel vision and lock in on your goals. However, overcommitment to a goal that truly isn't meant for you, that's not in alignment with what you actually want, or staying the course on a goal because of the sunk cost fallacy (feeling like you'll lose all you've invested if you turn back now... even though you have a gut instinct that you don't want this goal or you're only bringing half-ass effort to the goal) is a lose-lose situation.

Let's dive into how you'll know whether it's time to goal shift or time to stay the course on a goal.

When you're considering shifting, changing, or dropping a goal, there are a few questions you want to ask yourself before you make your decision:

➤ Am I wanting to shift, change, or drop this goal because it feels too hard... or because this is no longer a goal that I want to achieve?

➤ Is this goal in alignment with the season of life I'm in right now... or is this a goal from a past season that I continue to hold onto because I don't want to say I didn't achieve it?

➤ Was this a goal that I never really wanted (i.e. a goal that my parents or other people wanted for me and I went for it to please them)?

➤ Have I changed what I want?

➤ Do I no longer believe in my ability to get to the goal?

➤ Do I feel pulled in another direction?

➤ Do I think changing this goal will make achieving the next goal I set easier to do?

➤ Do I feel like this is too much work to go for the goal and I just don't have it in me to do it?

➤ Am I more addicted to the excitement of a new venture than the exhilaration of seeing a goal through to the end?

➤ Do I know how to work in the dark... or am I pursuing the goal so I get praise along the way?

➤ Do I believe I'm worthy of my highest good... or is my desire to shift the goal based on how worthy I feel in any given moment?

➤ What's more important to me- having what I want right now... or building the level of persistence, resilience, and grit that it takes to become a person who gets everything I want eventually?

Simply give yourself 30 minutes to an hour of quiet time. Sit with a journal and a pen. Go through each question and write down the answers your intuition sends your way. You'll know, from this self-exploration, if a goal you're pursuing is actually YOUR goal... OR... if it's a goal that needs to be adjusted, retired, or fired from your life.

If you go through this self-reflection and you come out feeling like "I still really want this goal but I'm afraid I won't be able to get there", then this is a goal that's coming from you and that is for you... and you've got to find a way to keep going. If you go through all of the reflection questions and you come out thinking "Yeah, I don't really know if that goal is what I really want for my life. I know I wanted it at some point... or maybe I didn't. But, right now, that goal doesn't feel right for me anymore", then it's time to goal shift because, even if you stay the course on that goal, because it's not in alignment with who you are and where you want to be, you won't go all in on achieving it... and you won't get to the finish line anyway. Before we get into how to goal shift, let me take a minute to talk about **Shiny Object Syndrome.** Shiny Object Syndrome (or SOS) is the tendency that all humans have to direct their time and focus to the new shiny object in their lives. This is especially true in the realm of goal achievement.

There's a feeling of exhilaration that comes with setting a new goal, starting a new project, or moving in a new life direction. That 'honeymoon phase' lasts until the decision has been made and now you're a little into doing the work. At some point, this 'new thing' no longer feels new. The 'new car smell' has worn off.

You're now into the roll-up-your-sleeves-and-do-the-work phase that represents the biggest part of the journey (and is also the most boring part). It's usually here where people start noticing new ideas, new goals, new dreams, new projects and their attention gets thrown onto the 'new' thing. At this point, people start to question the goal they're working on... especially when obstacles and challenges set in. If you find yourself goal hopping to the point where you've spent the last two or three years not achieving any major goals and simply starting a bunch of things that never get finished, rest assured- you are in Shiny Object Syndrome.

When I speak about goal shifting, I'm not talking about goal hopping. Goal shifting is about making a very intentional shift in an approach to a goal or in the goal itself because that goal no longer fits your life. When goal shifting is done well, you don't goal shift because you think the goal is 'too hard to achieve' or the work no longer keeps your interest. You goal shift because the goal no longer fits your life and, while you could keep investing in the goal and achieve it, it simply doesn't feel right for you.

You shift because there's a more pressing goal that needs your time and focus. But, when you goal shift, it's something that happens occasionally and not every time you find something new and exciting to pursue. That's the difference between what it feels like to shift a goal and what it feels like to fall prey to Shiny Object Syndrome.

Now that we're clear on the difference between goal shifting and Shiny Object Syndrome, let's talk about the steps to goal shifting. Effective goal shifting is done with intention. You begin by asking yourself "If not this goal, what goal really speaks to me?" You take the time to answer that in your journal. Typically, your intuition will give you an immediate answer. Be sure you write it down. For those of you who have spent years not tuning into your intuition, it may take more time in stillness. You may have to spend a few days getting reacquainted with your intuition and then ask the question to receive the answers.

Once you get clear on the goal (or goals) that really speak to you in this season of your life, you want to go through and assess the following:

- ✓ How important is this goal to the future I want to create?
- ✓ How much time, energy and money will I need to invest in pursuing this goal? And am I willing to give that?
- ✓ How on board are the people in my life with my achievement of this goal? Will they be supports to this goal... or will they (consciously or unconsciously) try to sabotage my achievement of the goal?
- ✓ If it were to take me 5 to 10 years longer to achieve this goal than I anticipate, would I still go after the goal?
- ✓ To what extent can I create joy and a sense of fulfillment on my way to this goal... or will the work of getting to the goal feel, most of the time, like a lot of heavy lifting?
- ✓ Who is my role model for this goal (a person who's already achieved this kind of goal or greater) and have I mapped out their path to get there so I'm not building my path from scratch?
- ✓ Am I really ready to go ALL IN on this goal?

If you come out of answering those questions feeling like "This IS the right goal for me and I'm ready to do whatever is required to achieve it", then it's time to make the unequivocal decision to goal shift to this new goal.

Here's an important point to note: The goal shifting **begins** by making the unequivocal decision to shift to this new goal. It does not end there. The entire process of goal shifting is both making the decision and following through on the Daily Massive Actions (DMAs) until you hit the point where taking the DMAs begin to feel natural. The moment your DMAs are on autopilot, you've made the total goal shift and you're now in "Get it done" mode. That's when you've completed the goal shifting process.

No matter what goals you are pursuing, understand that, in order to achieve any big goal, you have to get good at making it through the messy middle. The messy middle is most of the journey to any goal and it's the part of goal achievement that's monotonous and challenging. In times, it feels like walking through mud. You may not feel like you're making a bunch of progress in the messy middle and you have to stay focused on the fact that consistency of action is the marker of success through the messy middle, not the achievement of big milestones. The big milestones come as a result of staying the course.

When you're a person that needs the big milestones to keep going on a goal, you miss out on the entire purpose of going after the goal. The getting of the goal isn't the biggest reason to pursue it; it's the mastery of self-discipline that is the REAL purpose of doing the entire journey. When you become a person who follows through no matter what, it shifts your identity. You now become a person who, without a shadow of a doubt, keeps the commitments you make to yourself. You now become a person who, no matter what, has the level of focus, grit, and persistence required to achieve anything you set your mind to. That's why you go after big goals.

The passion of a goal is going to leave you very quickly at the beginning. Very soon after doing the same actions day after day, you're going to find yourself asking "Are we there yet?" That's normal. But, here's where you've got to dial in and stay focused. There are going to be moments, along the journey to the goal, where you're going to try to rationalize to yourself giving up on the goal. You're going to say things like "Is this really that important? Look how much I'm giving up right now to have this! Will this really matter in a year? What if this is costing me my health and my relationships? Is it really worth all of this?"

Your mind is exceptional at confirmation bias and, if you really want to give up on a goal, your mind will give you a thousand reasons why you should. Here's the ONE reason you shouldn't listen to any of that self-doubt conversation:

You said you'd do this and that's you giving your word to yourself. If you don't do this, you break your word to you… and that is the ULTIMATE form of self-betrayal.

Read that again because I really want you to feel, deep on the inside, what giving in to a self-doubt inner voice ALWAYS boils down to. Every time you give up on a goal because, in the moment, it feels easier to let the goal go than it would be to stay the course, you are making the achievement of the next goal that much harder because now you're going to have to fight an identity of self-betrayal that you keep strengthening with every goal you give up on.

Make no mistake: Giving up on your goal is not simply giving up on the goal; it's giving up on yourself… Sit with that… It's a very big price to pay that then leads you to have to double down and rebuild confidence as you go for the next goal.

Don't engage in it. Stay the course on the goals that matter to you. Keep your goals simple and stay connected to them on a daily basis… which is why writing out your goals every single day becomes so important. Have at least one goal in each of the four quadrants of life (health, wealth, spirituality, and relationships… and when you get super exhausted on the way to your goals (and you will), **learn to rest, not quit.**

It is helpful to feel the passion or be highly motivated to achieve your goals but it is not required. What is required for goal achievement is your ability to be committed, persistent, and remain laser focused on the decision you made to see this through... no matter what... and not simply because you said you would but because you know that you are worthy of whatever time it takes to achieve your biggest dreams.

Final Point: The achievement of every big goal is a massive lesson in patience. If patience is not a virtue for you (it certainly isn't for me), see the cultivation of patience along the goal journey as your opportunity to get an A in this spiritual classroom. You can do that... so do it...

And, as you live in this spiritual classroom, remember the words of Jm Storm:
"Patience is more than simply learning to wait. It is having learned what is worthy of your time." #readthatagain

CHAPTER 14: 10 QUESTIONS TO ASK YOURSELF WHEN PROGRESS HAS STALLED

Done is better than perfect.
- **Unknown**

There are going to multiple points, along the goal achievement journey, when progress will stall. It might stall for a few days, a few weeks, a few months, and possibly for a year. It's critical, especially if the stall in progress has been going on for more than a month, to get to the heart of it so you prevent it from moving into the territory of stalling for years.

What are the signs that progress on a goal has stalled?

<u>Here are 6 signs:</u>
- ➤ *Sign #1:* You stop writing out your goals daily (when you've built a habit of doing so).
- ➤ *Sign #2:* You go more than two weeks without taking action on a specific goal and you're more focused on putting out the 'daily fires' of life.
- ➤ *Sign #3:* Every time you sit down to work on the goal, you can't seem to get yourself to do the things you know you need to do (ex: staring at your laptop and feeling at a loss for what comes next).
- ➤ *Sign #4:* Every time you sit down to work on your goal, you feel like something or someone outside of you comes in to distract you from taking action on the goal (i.e. life seems to always get in the way).
- ➤ *Sign #5:* You are spending more time on things that don't get you closer to the goal (i.e. Netflix and chilling) rather than sticking to your focus blocks and doing work related to achieving the goal.
- ➤ *Sign #6:* You feel pessimistic about your ability to achieve the goal and keep thinking "What's the point of even trying?"

If any of the above six signs are present in your life, know that your goal progress has stalled. The question now becomes "How do you get unstuck?"

You begin by asking yourself (and answering) the following ten questions:

1. Where am I feeling stuck?
2. Why am I feeling stuck?
3. What led me to a place of making no or very little progress?
4. How hopeful do I feel about achieving my goal?
5. What could I do to increase my level of self-belief and self-trust in this goal journey?
6. Whose support would I like?
7. How can I go about asking for the support I now need?
8. What one next step would make me feel more confident about my progress on this goal?
9. When can I take this next step?
10. How will I celebrate my taking of this step?

Give yourself two to four hours to really sit with and answer those ten questions. They will point you in the direction of your best solutions. For example, if your goal progress is stalled because you don't feel like you're getting enough support from the people who live at home with you, the solution might be to have a boundary conversation and to clearly ask for specific kinds of support from the people closest to you. That may help you to honor and protect the time you spend working on your goals.

If, on the other hand, your progress has stalled because you're in a serious season of self-doubt and you live with this underlying belief that you never get to have what you want, the solution might be to identify one small action you can take every single day in your goal's direction. Intentionally stop and celebrate each day's win and use that to reinforce a new belief that you CAN have what you want and that you are getting closer to it.

Perhaps the stall in progress is because you're afraid of how your life will change once you achieve the goal. What if your friends or family will think you've changed, that you're acting like you're 'too good' for them? What if you worry that you won't have time for your kids because your level of goal achievement will require working so many more hours that you'll miss out on important matters?

These fears of "What if I get the goal but lose the people I love?" is a core, survival fear that most human beings have at one point or another. While it's easy to say "Well, that's not going to happen", when it's you pursuing a goal that you know will put you on an entirely new level of existence, one of the biggest fears that will come up is the fear of being rejected by those you love who only know you on this level. The solution to that might require working with a therapist or consistently having conversations with those you're worried about losing to A- reassure them that you want the relationship to grow and evolve as you do and B- to ask them to be proactive in sharing with you if they feel the relationship dynamics are changing in a way that isn't good. Again, the key is proactive and open communication.

The solutions to getting unstuck and back into making progress on your goals will be highly individual. You will know what solutions your stalled progress requires if you ask those ten questions and really listen for the answers.

From a generalist's approach, there are certain things that are going to help you get unstuck no matter what the cause of the progress stall.

Here are a few go-to solutions that will help you get unstuck and back into progress in most situations:

> **Gratitude.** What, in the pursuit of this goal, are you grateful for? What are you learning about yourself? How many opportunities have shown up for you? What are you excited about on this journey? Remember "The more you celebrate and praise your life, the more there is to celebrate." – Unknown

> **Optimism.** You can be a person who considers yourself "realistic" or even "pessimistic" but your attitude, about anything in your life, is up to you. You might not be naturally oriented to optimism but you can always decide to choose it. When a negative thought comes up about your goal, say to yourself "What's the optimistic take on that?" Create the optimist's view. Take on that viewpoint. Take your next step as you hold that viewpoint. Even if you're only able to hold an optimistic

viewpoint for ten minutes, use those ten minutes to take your next step.

➢ **Growth Mindset Language.** Shift how you talk about your goal journey. A growth mindset has a firm belief that, even if the current situation doesn't reflect the level of progress you want, you CAN change. You CAN learn. You may not have the results you want right now but that simply means you don't have the results YET. Notice the language in that. Using growth mindset language means going from "I should be doing this" to "I could be doing this", going from "I won't be able to handle that" to "I can handle that", shifting from "I don't know how to do that" to "I don't know how to do that… yet…" Hold yourself to using the growth mindset language and notice how you start to get unstuck simply with the words you say and speak to yourself…

➢ **Attitude Shift.** Adopt an "I don't' believe in defeat" attitude. This comes straight from Dr. Norman Vincent Peale's book <u>The Power of Positive Thinking</u> and let me give you his exact words so you understand how this works: "So the first thing to do about an obstacle is simply to stand up to it and not complain about it or whine under it but forthrightly attack it. Don't go crawling through life on your hands and knees half-defeated. Stand up to your obstacles and do something about them. You will find that they haven't half the strength you think they have." He goes on to quote the words of General Tudor "Just stand up to it, that's all, and don't give way under it, and it will finally break. You will break it. Something has to break, and it won't be you, it will be the obstacle." In other words, when obstacles show up (esp. when in the form of you not taking actions and procrastinating on working on the goal), say to yourself "I don't believe in defeat. I'm going to stop crawling through life on my hands and knees half-defeated. I'm not going to complain about the situation. **I'm going to HANDLE the situation.** Something in this situation has got to give and let's be clear- it will not be me. The obstacle will give because I'm not leaving until I handle this." Try saying that to yourself out loud ten times and see if you don't feel the re-energizing of your momentum.

One final point- no matter how much progress has stalled or how long you've been less than active on your goals, always come back to your WHY. Come back to why you're worthy of achieving this goal, why this goal MUST get achieved, and why, no matter what stands in the way, you WILL get through it. Remember that storms come to pass and that the only way to get beyond them is to go through them. Remember that you are stronger than your obstacles, wiser than anyone else's 'opinion' and capable of achieving great things. Keep those things in mind and find your way back on the path of taking Daily Massive Action (DMA). You CAN do that. Believe and then move in the direction of your greatest life...

CHAPTER 15: NEXT STEPS

You were born to win, but to be a winner, you must plan to win, prepare to win, and expect to win.
- Zig Ziglar

This book has provided a lot of information. You may have arrived at this chapter feeling overwhelmed and asking the question "Okay... So how do I take everything in this book and apply all of it?" The best answer I can give you is to take things one step at a time... which means Step #1 is you need a plan for taking action on the work of this book. I've created a massively helpful starter roadmap for you to implement everything you've learned in this book in the form of the Own Your Goals Planner Pack.

In this digital bundle, you'll receive a workbook containing an Own Your Goals Roadmap as well as a series of worksheets that move you through the steps covered in this book. It offers a step-by-step guide to truly owning your goals.

In addition to the worksheets, there's a walkthrough video that goes deeper on the what, when and how of applying the concepts in this book along with more case study examples that demonstrate what it looks like to go from goal setting to goal management to goal achievement. Be sure to click the link and check out the Own Your Goals Planner Pack.

As this book comes to a close, there are a few points I want to leave you with:
> - *Handle your self-belief FIRST.* Self-belief is the single most important determining factor of whether you are going to achieve your goal; don't substitute taking action for working on your level of self-belief. Self-belief comes first.
> - *Focus on consistency, not intensity.* A week of intense action will NEVER make up for the consistency of small actions taken every day for a long period of time. The frequency and consistency of your action taking is the #1 habit you need to develop to achieve any goal.

➤ *Redefine the importance of safety in your life.* Yes, safety matters but if wanting to 'be safe' is the thing that keeps you from taking the necessary risks to level up your life, your definition of safety has got to change. At the same time that you redefine your definition of safety, also redefine your definition of risk... and, whenever you feel like retreating back into an old definition of safety, remind yourself of this: "If you don't take risks, you will always work for someone who does." – Unknown #truestory

➤ *Go after your goals starting NOW.* I spent the entirety of <u>Stop Waiting For Permission: 42 Ways to Be the Powerful Creator of Your Best Life</u> talking about this exact thing. No more waiting... Don't wait for Monday, next week, or next year. You aren't promised to be here then. Go for what you want NOW... Doing this one thing alone sets a brand-new precedent in your life and will bring you closer to embodying your Future Self now.

➤ *Find a way to integrate joy and fulfillment in the journey.* This is the hardest one to do but the most important (after self-belief). Most of our lives will be spent on the journey to the next thing we want. If the only joy you have comes when you actually achieve the goal, you will miss your entire life waiting for a split second of happiness. Don't live that way. Make the ordinary extraordinary by making joy a non-negotiable in your EVERYDAY life.

If the goal you're going after is for you, BELIEVE that you already have everything you need WITHIN you to achieve it. But, then, don't sit on your laurels waiting to 'feel' like taking action. That will never happen. Once you know what you want, develop a plan and force yourself into immediate action on it. Make it so standard in your life that you get to a place where you take DMA (Daily Massive Action) without even thinking about.

I believe in you. It's time to believe in yourself... and act...

WOULD YOU LIKE TO KNOW MORE?

Seeing individuals step into their full power is one of my life purposes. I fulfill that mission in a number of ways and I invite you to join me on the journey.

Own Your Goals

Are you ready to create and achieve your most powerful goals? Would you like a step-by-step blueprint that will walk you through the process of setting and managing your life to goal success? The <u>Own Your Goals Planner Pack</u> is everything you need to truly own your goals. With a detailed roadmap, planner, worksheets, and a step-by-step roadmap, you'll have everything you need to take your goals from designed to done. Visit <u>https://www.kassandravaughn.com/ownyourgoalsplannerpack</u> to learn more about the <u>Own Your Goals Planner Pack</u>.

She Runs The Show

If you're a woman entrepreneur, an aspiring entrepreneur, or have any female friends who are thinking about entrepreneurship, invite them to join the movement on my iTunes podcast called She Runs the Show. You can find the latest episode at: <u>https://tinyurl.com/sherunstheshowpodcast</u>.

Stand in Your Power Audio Coaching Subscription

Are you ready for a powerful audio coaching subscription that will help you overcome self-doubt, grow your level of self-belief and create an amazing life? Check out the **Stand in Your Power Audio Coaching Subscription** at <u>www.kassandravaughn.com/standinyourpowersubscription</u>.

Looking for a speaker?

I love to facilitate workshops, lectures, and conference talks on the topics of focus, resiliency, grit, personal power, and self-worth. If you'd like to discuss my speaking at your event or creating a corporate workshop for your company, please contact me at <u>info@kassandravaughn.com</u>.

Check out my courses on Skillshare!

I've created a number of courses on Skillshare based on the topics that I coach, write, and speak about. Feel free to check out my courses on Skillshare at: https://www.skillshare.com/user/kassandravaughn.

Check out my other books

I love to write about overcoming fear and developing focus. Feel free to check out my other books at www.overcomingfearbooks.com.

If you have any questions, comments, or feedback, please email me at info@kassandravaughn.com.
I'd love to hear from you!

DID YOU LIKE THE BOOK?

If you liked the book, please recommend the eBook to friends, family, and any person you know who needs to read this. Also, please leave a review on Amazon and let me know how you felt about the book and what the book was able to help you accomplish. I'm always checking the reviews.

I'd love to respond to you personally. After you've left your Amazon review, please email me at info@kassandravaughn.com to let me know. Thanks in advance!

Kassandra